MW01240834

The Warmth Of The SON

Finding God in the Simple Moments of Life

Volume 3

TERRY HARRIS

Scripture taken from the Holy Bible, New International Version® © 1973, 1978.

ISBN – 13: 978-1541222939

ISBN – 10: 1541222938

Table of Contents

ACKNOWLEDGMENTS

I am so very grateful to two dear friends, Shelley Freeze, and Cynde Mutryn, for their inspiration for this book. A couple of years ago, they each came to me separately and told me they had been praying for God to touch my heart and give me the desire to put my weekly devotions into a book. These two ladies don't even know each other, so it was evident to me that God used them to speak clearly to me about His plan. After much encouragement and persistence on their parts, I am now trying to answer God's call obediently. This is volume 3 in the series.

I am forever grateful to my Lord and Savior, the God of the universe, for blessing me with a desire to write. This book is His, not mine. He alone gives me the words to say. He just uses me to write them down. There are so many times when I go back and look at something I wrote, and it almost seems unfamiliar to me. I ask myself, "Did I write that?" And I am reminded that God alone wrote it through me. I am completely humbled that He would do that and would use me to record His words of faith to us. Thank You, Lord!

I so appreciate my dear husband for his love, encouragement, prayers, and confidence in me as I have spent many hours writing and publishing, and I am grateful for his patience. He is one of God's greatest blessings to me.

Many thanks to our Tuesday-night prayer group for their continuous prayer and support of all my work as an author. I know it is only through the prayer of many that I was able to see this project to completion.

So many friends have encouraged me along the way with e-mails and comments about how the Lord spoke to them through my Thoughts for the Day, and I am so grateful for their support. My prayer is simply that God would use these devotions for His glory and bring many to a closer relationship with Him as a result. I am so grateful and thankful when I hear that He has done that.

The Lord brought me two wonderful people to fill in my "technology gap"—my editor, Libbye Morris, and my graphic designers, Kelly and Teresa Nielsen, who formatted the book for me. All used their wonderful expertise to make this book polished and ready for publishing. Thank you! I could not have done it without you.

> "I love your new book! I curled up with it as soon as I arrived home. Your stories really made me think about a lot of things, and also how to be more devoted to the Lord."
> — Donna P.

Preface

This is the third book in my series titled *The Warmth of the SON*. I would like to share with you the back story of this title.

One spring, I was experiencing a beautiful day on my patio. The sky was bright blue, and the warmth of the sun was toasty. To me it was the perfect day. I couldn't help but praise the Lord for His provision and His bright, happy sunshine as I sat there soaking up the warm sun on my body and face. I began to thank Him for this huge blessing, and immediately, the following poem came into my thoughts. It struck me how the *sun* is light, and the *Son* is light. The *sun* is warm, and at the same time, the *Son's* love is warm and kind. The *sun* can heal as we soak up vitamin D, and certainly the *Son* can heal us of many physical ailments and can also heal our soul of sin we harbor. The *sun* is bright, and so is the *Son*! Thank You, Lord, for the sun, and especially for Your *Son*!

As I was thinking of a title for this book series, I came upon this poem I had written, and it seemed to fit with my purpose for the book. As you read through my short stories, I pray that they will speak to you in a special way. And in the process, may the Son heal your soul, make you whole, fill your heart, and impart His love on you. In other words, may God use this book to speak to your soul and fill you with His overflowing love, grace, and mercy. That is my prayer.

Warmth of the SON

By Terry Harris

As I sit in the warmth of the sun
The warmth of the SON
Heals my soul.

As I sit in the warmth of the sun
The warmth of the SON
Makes me whole.

As I sit in the warmth of the sun
The warmth of the SON
Fills my heart.

As I sit in the warmth of the sun
The warmth of the SON
His love imparts.

1

No Fun in Funland

"In the same way your Father in heaven is not willing that
any of these little ones should be lost."
—Matthew 18:14

"I will search for the lost and bring back the strays. I will
bind up the injured and strengthen the weak."
—Ezekiel 34:16

"And hope does not disappoint us, because God has
poured out his love into our hearts by the Holy Spirit,
whom he has given us."
—Romans 5:5

For sixteen years, beginning when Stephanie was three years old
and Kim was five months, our family would spend a week each
summer in Rehoboth Beach, Delaware, near where I grew up.
It was always a fun week, very relaxing, and a time to rejuvenate
from the fast pace of city life and hectic schedules. Our girls
still talk of those times and the many wonderful memories that
were created there.

One of the things the girls loved most were our nightly visits
to Funland and going on all the rides. Funland was on the
boardwalk and had an assortment of different rides for many

different ages, from tiny toddlers to brave adults. Its popularity was unmatched, and during the peak summer months, the area would be a sea of people on any given evening. Funland was always filled with lots of families with wide-eyed young children who bore the excitement and wonder of it all. Sometimes you could hardly move, but that added to the exhilaration of it all.

However, we had a little more excitement one evening than we bargained for. That summer, Stephanie was five years old, and Kim was two. Stephanie was looking forward to riding on the carousel, and as John lifted her onto one of the horses and tightened the safety strap, Kim and I were standing right there watching Stephanie and seeing the joy and anticipation on her face. After John got Stephanie got situated and the carousel began to turn, I waved to her and then reached down to grab Kim's hand again. In that split second, she was gone!

I guess she got swept up in the movement of the crushing crowd, and her little body just moved along with them. John and I had panic attacks. A parent's worst nightmare had just come true for us. John ran one way, and I ran another. We raced through Funland for what felt like hours, all the while knowing that we had to get back to the carousel within a few short minutes to get Stephanie as her ride ended. I was sure I would never see my baby again! How could this be?

Finally, after searching and searching, I found Kim crying in the arms of a sweet "grandmotherly" lady! I cried, too. I can't tell you how overwhelming my relief and joy were. Thank you, Lord, for protecting my baby.

When I think of how much I love my children, it's hard to imagine that God loves us even more than that. Isn't that incredible? In fact, He loves us so much that He sent *His* own Son to die for our sins, becoming the ultimate sacrifice! Now that is an indescribable *love*!

Just my thought for the day…have a blessed one!

Abba Father, how can You truly love me *that much*? It is hard for me to imagine that kind of deep, abiding love. And thank You that when I am lost, You are not. You are there with me all the time. Amen.

My Thoughts

2

AWAKE ALL NIGHT!

"Therefore this is what the LORD says: 'If you repent, I
will restore you that you may serve me.'"

—Jeremiah 15:19

"I preached that they should repent and turn to God and
prove their repentance by their deeds."

—Acts 26:20b

"Godly sorrow brings repentance that leads to salvation
and leaves no regret, but worldly sorrow brings death."

—2 Corinthians 7:10

I will never forget a story my dear friend, Donna, told several
years ago when we and our husbands were in a Bible study
together. One particular evening, we were discussing the act
of praying to God in confession and repentance and asking for
His forgiveness.

As we all discussed this topic further and shared ways that
we have come before the Lord in confession, I will never forget
the story Donna told us about her experience one night when
she couldn't sleep. With humility, she shared with us that after
she went to bed, in her sleeplessness, thoughts of her failings
before the Lord and the wrongs that she had committed against

Him kept coming to mind. She felt these sins were clearly keeping her from being able to pray and were damaging her relationship with her heavenly Father. She knew that the only answer was to spend time discussing and confessing the times she had failed Him.

God sees all sin the same. Sin is sin, and although Donna definitely had not murdered anyone or robbed a bank, she had a clear understanding of the evil of *all* kinds of sin. She knew that, as Christians, we sometimes tend to minimize our sin by telling ourselves that it is not "too bad" or that we "didn't hurt anyone else." But all sin hurts God. And all sin is wrong.

So in the quiet of the night, she lay in bed in humble repentance before the Lord. She began with her obvious failings, and as she brought her sins before the Lord, He began to reveal even more areas where He wanted her to change. One by one, she confessed her sins to the Lord, baring her soul with a repentant heart. Her heart was heavy and her words to the Lord passionate and deep. As she named her sins one by one, her Lord and Savior heard her cries, and one by one He forgave her. She said that when she finally finished, it was after 2:00 a.m.! After that wonderful dedicated time with the Lord, she was able to fall asleep easily with her soul at peace.

I often think of that story and Donna's time with the King of kings. I remind myself that is exactly how the Lord wants me to come before Him—spending uninterrupted time in prayer and repentance. He wants me to spend lengths of time at His feet repenting and confessing and asking forgiveness. I sometimes think I confess and ask forgiveness without the appropriate depth and passion, and I need to use Donna's example to spend time with the Lord, focusing on nothing but my sin. The amazing power of what my dear friend did on that quiet night was surely life-altering and brought her closer to the Lord in the process. What a great example!

During that same discussion in our Bible study, another member of our group announced that sometimes it is hard to confess to Christians because so often, kind-hearted, sympathetic, empathetic believers come around the confessor to give hugs and kisses and basically say "That's OK" or "We've all done that" or something similar. How very wrong! The Bible clearly tells us otherwise. It will be good as Christians to treat sin in the way that God sees it, *lovingly* hold our fellow believers accountable like God tells us, and then come around them with support to help them, but not to tell them "It's OK."

Just my thought for the day…have a blessed one!

Dear Lord, sometimes I don't feel very lovable. In fact, because of my sin, sometimes I am certainly *not* lovable. But You love me anyway. And when I confess, You forgive me. That humbles me more than You can imagine. Thank You, Lord. Amen.

My Thoughts

3

LITTLE ANNOYANCES

"You are my hiding place; You will protect me from trouble."

—Psalm 32:7

"Consider it pure joy, my brothers, whenever you face trials of many kinds, because you know that the testing of your faith develops perseverance."

—James 1:2-3

"You will keep in perfect peace him whose mind is steadfast, because he trusts in you. Trust in the LORD forever, for the LORD, the LORD, is the Rock eternal."

—Isaiah 26:3-4

One evening, my husband and I were attending a business event in Washington, DC, and it was fairly late when we left to return home. My husband has an impeccable sense of direction and has lived in and around DC his entire life. He can find places that exasperate even the most seasoned natives. But even with that, somehow we took a wrong turn, which then caused us to get lost temporarily, although my husband would not call it "lost." He agrees with our daughter, who likes to proclaim, "You are never lost…you're always *somewhere*!"

We ended up going out of our way by about twenty minutes

until we found the correct road back and got on track again. Because it was already pretty late, we were a bit annoyed at the fact that we would now arrive home even later than we had planned. In fact, we were so annoyed that we started grumbling all the way back home.

Once back on our regular route and a few miles down the road, we came upon a very bad multicar accident; one car was evidently hit by an oncoming vehicle. As we sat there waiting for the accident to be cleared so we could continue, it was easy to again be a bit annoyed until it occurred to me that this accident had just happened…maybe about twenty minutes earlier! This could have been *our* car. It could have been *our* accident! Did God use our wrong-turn delay to help us avoid being in this accident? We will never know.

I believe that our annoyances at things that cause us delay should not be considered annoyances. I believe God often uses those delays to protect us. And for that I am very grateful. We have all heard the stories of September 11th in which many who worked in the Twin Towers were delayed in getting to work that day by little annoyances…traffic problems, children not being ready on time to leave for school, and cars breaking down. Those people were spared because of those "little annoyances."

My prayer is that I will always thank God for these little annoyances, for the delays in my schedule and in my life and for those who make me "wait". I never know if God is using those to protect me. And I am grateful.

Just my thought for the day…have a blessed one!

Heavenly Father, I am so very grateful for Your protection today and every day. Help me trust You more, and forgive my complaining about life's annoyances. Amen.

My Thoughts

4

THE SNOW TRAIN

"Be still, and know that I am God."

—Psalm 46:10

"I have told you these things, so that in me you may have peace. In this world you will have trouble. But take heart! I have overcome the world."

—John 16:33

"For God is not a God of disorder but of peace."

—1 Corinthians 14:33

Each year when we enjoy the white, icy snow that blankets our area, I am reminded of how my brother and I used to go sledding as children. In fact, many in the town where we grew up did this. We lived in southern Delaware, where the biggest hill was the little ant hill in the backyard. But when it snowed, we had the time of our lives sledding. We didn't need a big hill, or even a small one, because we had a special "flat land" technique for enjoying a sleigh ride.

In the evening, after a snowstorm ended and had dropped several inches on the ground, all the families in our neighborhood would bundle up in all their snow gear, the dads would bring the sleds and long rope out of the sheds and basements, and one family car would be selected.

Then, with the car in the street, the dads would begin tying all the sleds together and tie the "train" to the car. I know, I know…you're saying, "What if someone got hurt! Heavens, don't you know this is an accident waiting to happen?" Well, actually, not. This was a small town, and back in the day, people took responsibility and worked hard to ensure their *own* safety. We never had one accident while participating in this "unsafe" activity. And neither did anyone else in our town. But we surely did have fun!

These sledding events always took place at night, after dinner. People were not out "going places" at night after a snowfall… *unless*, of course, they were car sledding! It was cold, and it was very quiet, with only the glow of the streetlights to illuminate the bright white, freshly fallen snow. Because the land was flat, and because the driver went very slowly, and because each sled had one adult on it, we were all safe and happy kids. We laughed, and we sang. We drove through the town, sometimes passing other cars with sled "trains" attached to them, too, and we would all wave and scream with joy and delight. In fact, the only cars that were out were the ones pulling sleds! Looking back, I think it was truly the most fun I had as a child.

As we would travel around town on our sled train, the thing that struck me was how quiet, very quiet, the town was. No one was out, the snow had just fallen, and the street lights cast a golden glow across the land. It was serene, and it was beautiful. There was a peacefulness that I never experienced at any other time. I think, even as a child, I felt the peaceful presence of God during those evenings. I was in awe, and at the same time,

I felt an inexplicable calm and peace, so close to God. Even now, I get that same feeling when I remember our sled-train experience.

Just my thought for the day…have a blessed one!

Lord, I know that peace comes only from You. Thank You, that even amidst the chaos or dysfunction around me, I can rely on You to give me a spirit of peace. Amen.

My Thoughts

5

OVERFLOWING

"Give, and it will be given to you. A good measure, pressed down, shaken together and running over, will be poured into your lap. For with the measure you use, it will be measured to you."

—Luke 6:38

"How great is the love the Father has lavished on us, that we should be called children of God!"

—1 John 3:1

"For I am convinced that neither death nor life, neither angels nor demons, neither the present nor the future, nor any powers, neither height nor depth, nor anything else in all creation, will be able to separate us for the love of God that is in Christ Jesus our Lord."

—Romans 8:38–39

Recently my husband and I spent some alone time with our young grandson while our daughter was taking our granddaughter to an appointment. It was fun to have Grandma and Grandpa time with him, hear about his day at school, and talk about the sports he loves, as well as all the things that are important to a six-year-old. We needed to get some lunch, so we took him to a fast-food restaurant nearby.

After placing our orders, and while my husband was waiting for the order to be filled, I went with our grandson to get our drinks at the machine. I filled the first cup with ice, put it under the soda dispenser, and pushed the button. The cup filled nearly to the top, and I released my finger from the button. But the soda keep pouring out! The button was stuck, and try as I might, the soda would not stop flowing!

I pushed the button harder…click, click, click. Nothing! The soda was coming full force out of the machine, overflowed the cup, and started filling up the trough underneath. It wouldn't be long before it overflowed that, too.

By now I was feeling a bit panicked and totally embarrassed because I was sure that everyone in the restaurant was looking my way. I pushed and pushed the button, but it was so jammed that the soda continued to pour at breakneck speed out of the dispenser. I was powerless to stop it! It was a horrible feeling. I called for help. The manager came out and hit some emergency button on the side of the machine, which I think he had done several times before, and that stopped the chaos so that finally the waterfall of soda ceased. I made some comment about not *really* being that thirsty.

Once everything got back to normal, I couldn't help but think of the Scripture verse in Luke 6:38, in which Jesus speaks of how much God will give us when we freely give to others. I could not stop the flow of soda, and neither can I ever stop the everlasting love of Jesus after I have given my life and heart to Him. Isn't it amazing how much the Father loves us and showers us with His love, mercy, grace, and forgiveness?

Just my thought for the day….have a blessed one!

Heavenly Father, You are my all in all, my one and
only, my life support! Thankfully, when I need
You most, You are there to pour freely on me Your
mercy, grace, and love. You never stop pouring it
out upon me. Thank You, Lord! Amen.

My Thoughts

6

ROCKIN' SEAS AND QUEASY KNEES

"During the fourth watch of the night Jesus went out to them, walking on the lake. When the disciples saw Him walking on the lake, they were terrified. 'It's a ghost,' they said, and cried out in fear. But Jesus immediately said to them, 'Take courage! It is I. Don't be afraid.' 'Lord, if it's You,' Peter replied, 'tell me to come to You on the water.' 'Come,' he said. Then Peter got down out of the boat, walked on the water and came toward Jesus. But when he saw the wind, he was afraid and, beginning to sink, cried out, 'Lord, save me!' Immediately Jesus reached out his hand and caught him. 'You of little faith,' he said, 'why did you doubt?'"

—Matthew 14:25–31

"Now faith is being sure of what we hope for and certain of what we do not see."

—Hebrews 11:1

It is absolutely no fun being on a rocking ship! Well, maybe it's fun for the first few hours, as you laugh yourself silly because you can't walk straight without holding onto something or you watch in awe as your soup sloshes from side to side in the soup bowl at dinner. Or maybe even taking a shower is a humorous challenge as you try to hold onto the railing while at the same time lathering up your body with your soapy washcloth and then rinsing off!

In the fairly recent past, my husband and I were blessed to be able to go on a cruise with some friends. It was a wonderful adventure, especially after the ship finally docked in Bermuda! I am not one to get seasick. I grew up on the water near beaches and spent many hours on boats of all kinds. Thankfully, only once did I ever get seasick, and that was because of what I ate before sailing. However, this trip to Bermuda was a different experience.

A hurricane had come up the East Coast just prior to our excursion on the seas, and in its wake, it left some pretty "rockin' waters." At first it was hilarious because I couldn't walk in a straight line without holding onto a railing or to someone's arm. We all looked a little silly getting from here to there as we walked to meals and shows. But we quickly got used to it and learned to compensate for the ship's sassy dance on the seas. I remember at meals looking out the window, first to see the view of the churning waters below and then, a few seconds later, to see the bright blue sky above! Up and down we went.

But by the second day, the novelty wore off for me, and it was a bit less funny. In fact, I even began to feel queasy, and my stomach wished for a nonrocking place to reside. I began counting the hours until we docked and stabilized so that my brain and my stomach could stop rocking to some unknown jiving tune. Even though I never actually got sick, I came pretty close by the time we arrived in Bermuda.

The rough seas on our trip and the up and down of the

rocking boat reminded me of what we sometimes go through in our spiritual lives…the ups and the downs of life and how sometimes it even seems hard to walk in a straight spiritual line without holding on. There are times when the waves seem to whip around us, knock us off balance, and threaten to engulf us. It is unrelenting. Spiritual warfare can be brutal, and we beg God for relief. Sometimes God brings relief quickly, and other times He allows us to stay in the storm while He walks with us, holding us and encouraging us.

It reminds me of Peter when he got out of the boat to walk toward Jesus. The minute he took his eyes off the Lord, Peter began to sink. Sometimes our circumstances are so overwhelming that we find it difficult, if not impossible, to keep looking at Jesus. For me, it's so easy just to keep going back to my difficulties. But if I can keep my eyes on Jesus instead of the storm around me, what a difference it makes! That is the key to the stability of my life.

Just my thought for the day…have a blessed one!

Dear Lord, it happens every time. The minute I take my eyes off You, my life begins to fall apart. May I always have eyes only for You, Lord. Amen.

My Thoughts

7

You Can't Take It with You

"'Though your riches increase, do not set your heart on them."

—Psalm 62:10b

"For where your treasure is, there your heart will be also."

—Matthew 6:21

"Honor the LORD with your wealth, with the firstfruits of all your crops."

—Proverbs 3:9

"Wealth is worthless in the day of wrath, but righteousness delivers from death."

—Proverbs 11:4

We have all heard that phrase "You can't take it with you," and we each have probably said it many times. I know I have. Well, the other day I saw an interesting picture someone had taken. It was a picture of a large, beautiful, white hearse, evidently bearing a loved one who had passed away. Maybe it was going to the cemetery. Or to the church.

However, upon closer observation, I noticed something else in the picture. The hearse was pulling a U-Haul trailer! The caption of the picture read, "Apparently, you *can* take it with you!" That picture and caption are hilarious, but of course, as we all know, they don't allow U-Hauls in heaven!

As I really pondered that scene and looked at it a bit more seriously, I realized many important aspects of it. How many times have I held tightly onto my money and my things rather than use them to honor God or to bless others? I am certainly guilty.

In the move my husband and I recently experienced, we downsized by moving into a smaller home. Because I have always been eager to get rid of my unnecessary "things," the decluttering process was fairly easy for me. However, God did use this move to help me personally apply the downsizing mentality to my heart as I went through the process of making some tough choices about certain items. And He helped me realize that at this time in my life, having less to care for and maintain is an especially good thing. It is very freeing.

In their recent retirement and move, my brother and sister-in-love downsized from a four-bedroom home to a two-bedroom and den condo, and their example solidified our move in my mind. They love the condo concept because they say, for them, instead of having to spend hours maintaining a home with lawn care and home maintenance, they felt it freed them up for more time to serve the Lord by serving others in their new town.

And in our retirement years, as well, my husband and I realize that we also don't want to spend endless hours taking care of things. We have spent a lifetime doing that. I also discovered that I would rather spend more time helping people, being involved in our church, and making a difference in the town

God moved us to. Does that mean that, to do that, I have to live in a one-room hut and give away all my clothes? Of course not! But I came to realize that I can truly live with many fewer things in my life and still be very, very happy.

While everyone's situation is different, in our situation with our move, God clearly spoke to me regarding my things, and the result has been freedom, joy, and more time to do the activities that matter to me…and to God.

Just my thought for the day…have a blessed one!

Lord, help me to always separate my needs from my wants and to want *You* and *Your* will more than anything. Amen.

My Thoughts

8

THE NAUSEATING GREEN WALLS

"Let us fix our eyes on Jesus, the author and perfecter of our faith, who for the joy set before him endured the cross, scorning its shame, and sat down at the right hand of the throne of God."

—Hebrews 12:2

"But the fruit of the Spirit is love, joy, peace, patience, kindness, goodness, faithfulness, gentleness and self-control."

—Galatians 5:22-23

The psalmist says in Psalm 118:24, "This is the day the LORD has made; let us rejoice and be glad in it." I wake up each morning rejoicing in the Lord, for His gift of a new day. Before I even bound out of bed, I like to thank Him for the gift of a brand-new day of life and a new day to experience His love, His creation, and the love of my family and friends. But I have to be honest with you—there are some days when I have difficulty rejoicing.

Recently there was a day like that. The remodeling of our home that we had purchased near our daughter and grandchildren was nearing completion. Although it was becoming obvious that it would not be fully completed by moving day, it would be close enough that we could move our furniture in, and the final areas could be finished around it. We would live at our daughter's house for a couple of weeks until everything was done.

In the midst of all this, we needed to be out of town for a weekend. It wasn't really a great time to be away because whenever construction is going on, we know from past experience that we need to be there and available on a daily basis. Sometimes last-minute decisions need to be made. So, as you can imagine, it was during this short time span that everything that could fall apart did.

The installation of the ceramic tile in the master bath was completed incorrectly on a Friday, in part due to a lack of communication between us and the contractor. Thankfully, our daughter went down to the house that evening to see what had been completed that day and noticed the gross error. Because of the way it was installed, the installer ran out of certain tiles and had an overabundance of others. Thankfully, the contractor called the installer, and he was able to come back that evening, remove the tiles that had not yet dried, and complete the job as planned.

Then on Sunday night, we got a call from our daughter, who had again gone down to the house earlier to see how things were progressing. When she walked in the door and looked at the entryway, living room, dining area, and hallway that were supposed to be painted a soft, creamy yellow, she nearly got sick. Instead of that soft, creamy color, those walls were all painted a dark, ugly, repulsive, and nauseating shade of green!

It was so horrific that I am convinced they shouldn't even *make* that color!

How could that possibly happen? After going to my "house notebook" where I kept notes on virtually everything associated with our move and project, I saw it. When I had typed out a list for the painter with the paint colors for all the rooms, I listed the correct paint *name*, but I had transposed the last two digits of the four-digit *number*! I guess the paint store goes by number only. How can two little numbers make such a huge difference? I was just sick—not because the paint was such a yucky color, but because I had caused so much extra work for the men who had been working so hard on our behalf to meet our schedule. I had not only caused them extra labor but had caused the project to slow down for them. I felt just terrible. How could I have been so careless and irresponsible?

As I read my *Jesus Calling* devotional that day, I realized the answer. I must keep my eyes on Jesus, even during the crises of the day. He alone must be my focal point. As Sarah Young says in this wonderful little book, "Make Me your focal point as you move through this day…circumstances are in flux, and the world seems to be whirling around you. The only way to keep your balance is to fix your eyes on Me, the One who never changes." Thank you, Sarah Young, for reminding me today!

Just my thought for the day…have a blessed one!

My gracious Father, may I always keep my eyes on You and not on my circumstances. You provide order and peace to my soul when I keep my focus on You. Amen.

My Thoughts

9

THE TRIP THAT
ALMOST WASN'T

"A gift given in secret soothes anger."

—Proverbs 21:14

"For it is by grace you have been saved, through faith –
and this not from yourselves, it is the gift of God – not by
works, so that no one can boast."

—Ephesians 2:8–9

"Every good and perfect gift is from above, coming down
from the Father of the heavenly lights, who does not
change like shifting shadows."

—James 1:17

A few years ago, when I owned my own scrapbooking business,
each August I would pack up my suitcase and head from
Washington, DC, to the Midwest for several fun-filled, high-
energy days of learning, celebrating, and being motivated. It
was a joy to meet with my team and friends from across the
country at our annual National Convention in Minnesota.

One particular year, a close business friend decided to come
down to Washington, DC, to fly to Minnesota with me. This
promised to be a wonderful time together, and because we did

not see each other that often, we would have fun catching up on our personal lives and what our families were doing, as well as make some business plans and share ideas.

We decided that the easiest way to get to the airport would be the DC subway, called the Metro. My husband took us to the nearest Metro station and dropped us off, and we eagerly hurried to the train platform after securing our tickets in the automatic ticket machine. As we stood waiting for our train, we shared our excitement for not only the trip, but all the wonderful fun-filled events at convention. As the train approached and we boarded, we continued our conversation.

We still had plenty of time before our flight took off, so we sat back in our Metro seats, relaxed, and watched station after station pass by. Soon we would be at the end of the line at Reagan National Airport, and we couldn't wait. As we continued chattering away in deep conversation, without warning, the conductor blared through the speaker, "End of line...Navy Yard!"

What? Navy Yard? We were supposed to be at Reagan National Airport!

As we got off the train and looked, we realized that we had boarded the wrong train at Metro Center, where we had transferred. We were just a little frustrated, but with hope and perseverance, we got on the train to head back to Metro Center. We got off the train again, waited on the platform, and then boarded the *correct* train, which came soon. We were once again on our way to the airport.

My friend and I laughed and chatted about our crazy experience and how silly it was to board the wrong train. What were we thinking? In fact, we talked and talked all the way to the end of the line, where we once again heard the conductor say, "End of line…*Navy Yard*!"

Oh, my gosh! We just could not believe that we had been so incredibly engrossed in our conversations that we had made the mistake not once, but *twice*! This time, as we were heading back to Metro Center, my friend looked at her watch and announced that we were indeed now missing our flight!

Thankfully, we did finally manage to get ourselves to the airport, get our flights changed, and get to Minnesota. But this story has gone down in history as being one of the most incredulous, and shall we say not-so-intelligent things, we have ever done.

Have you ever missed something in life? Maybe you have been so engrossed in all the stresses and pressures of life that you are missing God's gifts to you. That has certainly happened to me, too. In addition to missing a flight, I have sometimes missed the beauty of what is going on around me because I am so busy. Or I'm so absorbed in my own little world that I fail to notice that God has put someone in my path who needs help or is lonely. What a blessing it is to help someone. It's easy to do that when we are paying attention. And what a sad thing to not notice the gifts that God brings to us to bless us each day.

Just my thought for the day…have a blessed one!

My dear heavenly Father, You give me so many gifts. Forgive me, Lord, for the times that I am too distracted, too self-absorbed, and too selfish to notice them, and I miss the blessings and gifts You have for me. Amen.

My Thoughts

10

Work as Unto the Lord

"And whatever you do, whether in word or deed, do it all in the name of the Lord Jesus, giving thanks to God the Father through him."

—Colossians 3:17

"I can do everything through him who gives me strength."

—Philippians 4:13

"Do everything without complaining or arguing."

—Philippians 2:14

I grew up in Delaware near our favorite summertime place, Rehoboth Beach. For many years, my grandmother managed the Rehoboth Beach Bath House, where people who came to the beach only for the day could have a place to change into their bathing suits, put their clothes in a locker, shower at the end of the day, and change back into clothes. As a child, I would often help my grandmother during the summer in the bath house by cleaning, renting out lockers, and doing whatever else was needed. This was one of the things that helped me develop a strong work ethic and a desire to help others.

When I think back to those times, I realize how hard my grandmother worked in her later years of life. I would stay with her in the tiny cottage she rented, which had one little living room, a small bedroom, and an even tinier kitchen. After a very long day of work, we would have to clean the bath house, search the beach for all the bathers who refused to honor the "Close at 6:00 p.m. sharp" sign, lock up the bath house, and walk several blocks back to the cottage.

My grandmother was a tiny lady, and she would put all the cash receipts into a small suitcase and carry them back to the cottage. We would shower, change into fresh summer clothes, go out to dinner or fix it at the cottage, and then she would take me to Funland, where I could ride all the rides and play the games. I realize now how late we must have gotten home and how tired she must have been. But she was always faithful to "reward" me for my day of work.

After coming back to the cottage and getting ready for bed, we would say prayers, she would tuck me in, and then she would go into the little kitchen and sit up for a long time, counting and recording the receipts from the day, preparing the deposit to take to the bank early the next morning as we walked back to the bath house. She did this all summer long and never once complained. She had to be exhausted, but she did her work as unto the Lord.

I learned many things from my grandmother during those summers. She taught me how to work hard without complaining, how to focus on others while serving them, how to think of others before myself, how to work before playing, and how to serve the Lord.

I am very grateful for those life lessons, and I am grateful for a grandmother who loved the Lord and shared His love with me every day by her example. We had many times of laughter and joy as we worked as unto the Lord.

Just my thought for the day…have a blessed one!

Lord, some days I am just so tired that it is hard to even think of work. During those times, please give me an extra measure of strength and help me to not complain but instead to thank You for my ability to do work, especially work that blesses others. Amen.

My Thoughts

11

GREEN STAMPS AND CRUNCH

"Christ redeemed us from the curse of the law by becoming a curse for us, for it is written: 'Cursed is everyone who is hung on a tree.' He redeemed us in order that the blessing given to Abraham might come to the Gentiles through Christ Jesus, so that by faith we might receive the promise of the Spirit."

—Galatians 3:13–14

"But when the time had fully come, God sent his Son, born of a woman, born under law, to redeem those under law, that we might receive the full rights of sons."

—Galatians 4:4–5

"In him we have redemption through his blood, the forgiveness of sins, in accordance with the riches of God's grace that he lavished on us with all wisdom and understanding."

—Ephesians 1:7–8

"For he has rescued us from the dominion of darkness and brought us into the kingdom of the Son he loves, in whom we have redemption, the forgiveness of sins."

—Colossians 1:13–14

Back in the day, when I was a young child, I remember S&H Green Stamps. If you are as old as I am, you probably remember them, too. As I recall, when you shopped at various stores, you were given a certain number of stamps, green in color, depending on the total amount of your purchase, and as you collected them, you licked the back of the stamps and stuck them in a little booklet. When the booklet was filled with stamps, you could take it to the redemption center to pick out a gift, which could be anything from little decorative items to kitchen utensils. Some items required more than one book.

I remember my mother, and seemingly every other mother in town, diligently and faithfully collecting their Green Stamps and adding them to their booklets each time they purchased from a store that offered the stamps. My mother saved them for a long time, it seemed, because she needed a new lamp, and she had seen one at the redemption center that she wanted to get. I even remember going with her to the center, and she was thrilled to pick out her special lamp to take home. As we stood at the counter, I watched her hand over her full booklets of hard-earned stamps to redeem them for her beautiful lamp.

That booklet had a great value placed on it because it represented a significant dollar amount with which to "purchase" something special. I think my mother redeemed stamps for other items at the Green Stamp store along the way, but I specifically remember the lamp.

To me, the Green Stamp collection was the adult version of children collecting box tops from cereal to redeem them for a valued toy puzzle, a decoder ring, or other coveted childhood toy. I vividly remember how much I loved to eat Rice Krispies cereal as a young child—not so much for the love of the crunch, but for the new puppet I received from saving many box tops. I can't remember if I was the proud owner of Snap, Crackle, or Pop, but I do remember the day I mailed in my box tops to redeem them for my amazing puppet. And the day the mailman arrived, package in hand, I was one happy child!

As I look back over these wonderful memories, I realize that long before my mother redeemed her Green Stamps for a lamp, and I redeemed my cereal box tops for a puppet, there was a much more important redemption that took place. Jesus redeemed us by giving His life for our sins! He loves us so very much that He redeemed us, bought us, by shedding His blood and dying on the cross for us.

There is no way we can achieve salvation on our own by obeying laws and doing good works. God knew that a sacrifice needed to be made to bridge the huge chasm between us and Him because of our sin, and that sacrifice was His precious and only Son, Jesus. God loves us so much that He was willing to do that for us…give up His Son to die on our behalf. And for that, those of us who have given our lives to Him are eternally grateful.

Just my thought for the day…have a blessed one!

How can I begin to thank You, Lord, for the gift
of Your Son? I have life eternal because of Him. It
is so hard to even imagine. Amen.

My Thoughts

12

RED SKY AT NIGHT

"The Pharisees and Sadducees came to Jesus and tested him by asking him to show them a sign from heaven. He replied, 'When evening comes, you say, 'It will be fair weather, for the sky is red, and in the morning, today will be stormy, for the sky is red and overcast.' You know how to interpret the appearance of the sky, but you cannot interpret the signs of the times.'

—Matthew 16:1–3

"Where morning dawns and evening fades you call forth songs of joy."

—Psalm 65:8b

It *had* to be a fire! As I was sitting in my upstairs home office working early in the evening, I turned to look out the window, which faces west. I saw what looked like vast flames behind the houses across the street. It looked as though the entire neighborhood was on fire! The most vibrant deep burnt orange and yellow flames arose high in the air and covered the entire sky. The flames flickered and seemed to lap at the blue sky like a cat lapping up the milk in his bowl. They were preparing to engulf everything nearby—the trees, the homes, and all in their path.

And then reality hit me: these were not flames at all! Our neighborhood was not on fire, and fire was not roaring past the houses consuming everything in sight. It was a sunset! A most extraordinary sunset and a beautiful example of God's creation.

A friend used to recite the rhyme "Red sky at night, sailor's delight; red sky in the morning, sailors take warning." I, too, have recited that for years. Sometimes people roll their eyes at me as I sincerely use that as a predictor of the weather for the next day, and I assure them that it truly works!

Even though I don't think anyone has really taken me seriously, I have persevered with my little rhyme. And then one day when I was reading my Bible, there it was! It wasn't my friend who made up that rhyme, but Jesus! He told the Pharisees and Sadducees, right there in Matthew 16, how the colors in the sky actually foretell what the weather will be! I feel so validated. All along, I have been repeating what *Jesus* said.

Isn't it amazing the truths we find in the Bible? Not only the truths of the Gospel and the many promises of God, but even simple things like knowing how to read the weather through God's creation. There is so much to be learned in the Scriptures. God put every single sentence and every single word in the Bible for a specific purpose. Now it's up to us to read every single sentence and every single word to know specifically what God is telling us.

The next time you see a red sky in the morning or in the evening, you will know that long before you heard that little rhyme, Jesus confirmed those words to the Pharisees and Sadducees. In so doing, He reminded us forever that God is in control of the weather every day.

Just my thought for the day...have a blessed one!

Lord, I am continually in awe of Your awesomeness! You bless me daily with Your spectacular creation, which shows me just how much You love me. Thank You, Lord. Amen.

My Thoughts

13

STOVE EXPLOSION!

"Humble yourselves before the Lord, and he will lift you up."
—James 4:10

"When pride comes, then comes disgrace, but with humility comes wisdom."
—Proverbs 11:2

"Let the wise listen and add to their learning."
—Proverbs 1:5

Back when I was in high school, girls always took a home economics class. Today I think they call it "home arts" or something similar, and guys, as well as girls, take the class. That's a good thing.

On one particular day in home economics class, our teacher was instructing us on how to light the gas ovens so we could bake the cakes we were making. My class was divided into four groups, and that's because we had four stoves, all gas. I had never cooked on a gas stove because at home we had electric. We all listened dutifully to our teacher as she explained in great detail how to light the oven. We were to open the oven door, light a match, and then turn the knob to begin the flow of gas. Once we held the match over the little hole at the bottom of the oven, the flame would ignite the gas, and *voilà*! The oven would begin heating.

Simple enough, right? Well, for some reason the girls in my group designated me to light our oven. I was probably the only one who did not have a gas stove at home, so this did not make sense. But I think our teacher had managed to scare everyone enough about the risks and following instructions explicitly that they all decided they wanted no part of this little project. So, as the one with absolutely no experience, they chose me.

With complete confidence, but not with complete memory, I proceeded. First I opened the oven door and turned on the gas. Next, I strolled across the classroom, looked for and finally found a box of matches, and then strolled back to our stove. I know…you're way ahead of me here. How did I get these instructions so *out of order*? Then I proceeded to lean over the open oven door and light the match!

What happened next caused the teacher and the entire class to come running to our little station. The sound of the explosion was so loud that I'm surprised the *entire school* didn't come running. I was in stunned shock. What in the world just happened? I can tell you what happened…I had a quick lesson in how not to light a gas stove! Praise God that no one was hurt or injured. At this point, I was totally embarrassed—mortified, really—about my lack of expertise. Actually, it was more a lack of following explicit instructions and of having a prideful attitude. I learned quickly that I needed to pay attention, humble myself, and follow instructions *completely*.

Being humble is a good thing. In fact, it's how God expects believers to act—with humility. In 1 Peter 5:5, He tells us,

"Clothe yourselves with humility toward one another, because God opposes the proud but gives grace to the humble." God cannot stand pride in us. God says in Proverbs 8:13, "I hate pride and arrogance." Humility helps us be gentle of heart and more like Jesus. And being more like Jesus is always a good thing!

Just my thought for the day…have a blessed one!

Heavenly Father, I do truly want to be more like Your Son, Jesus. It's not always an easy thing to do. No, it's actually a very hard thing to do! That's why I have to try so hard every minute of every day. Thank You, Lord, for guiding me and loving me. Amen.

My Thoughts

14

Books of Blessings

"I will make a covenant of peace with them and rid the land of wild beasts so that they may live in the desert and sleep in the forests in safety. I will bless them and the places surrounding my hill. I will send down showers in season; there will be showers of blessing."

—Ezekiel 34:25–26

"Blessed is the man who perseveres under trial because when he has stood the test, he will receive the crown of life that God has promised to those who love him."

—James 1:12

"Be joyful always; pray continually; give thanks in all circumstances, for this is God's will for you in Christ Jesus."

—1 Thessalonians 5:16–18

When our grandchildren were six and eight years old, I gave them tiny little notebooks and pens because I knew they loved to write things down, make lists, and record things they deemed important. As they were leaving our house to go home with our daughter, I talked with them about how they could use the notebooks to write down one blessing each day before going to bed.

I said that before they have their devotions, which our daughter faithfully does with them each evening, they could write down the date and then write their biggest blessing for that day. I even told them that I would be doing the same thing and that we could share our blessings when they came to visit or spend the night with us.

Our precious little Madison looked at me with her questioning, yet sincere, eight-year-old eyes and said, "But Mom-Mom, what if some days there are no blessings?" As adults, I know there are days where we certainly feel like that. Days where the problems have been so huge, the pain has been so deep, or the exhaustion so great that it feels as though there has not been one blessing, nothing on which to hang our gratitude sign that day. And I'm sure that to Madison it feels that way some days, too.

However, I assured our grandchildren that there is *always* a blessing, but sometimes we have to look for it. And some days we have to look harder than others to find it. So, to make sure that "blessings" didn't get confused with and become synonymous with "things I want," I reminded them that often a blessing can be something like a beautiful sunset, a fun, deep snow, having food to eat that day, or enjoying a hug from Mommy.

In this conversation, Madison reminded me that I have to check my heart each day and make sure I am grateful to the Lord for the *many* blessings He bestows on me and my family. Keeping a gratitude journal is going to help me do that and help me keep my focus on the Lord, not on my circumstances.

Just my thought for the day…have a blessed one!

My dear heavenly Father, some days I just seem to have run out of gratitude! Instead, I get an attitude. I am so very sorry, Lord. Help me with my attitude adjustment. Amen.

My Thoughts

15

ALCOHOL ATTACK

"Finally, be strong in the Lord and in his mighty power. Put on the full armor of God, so that you can take your stand against the devil's schemes. For our struggle is not against flesh and blood, but against the rulers, against the authorities, against the powers of this dark world and against the spiritual forces of evil in the heavenly realms."

—Ephesians 6:10–12

"The LORD gives strength to his people; the LORD blesses his people with peace."

—Psalm 29:11

"Therefore put on the full armor of God, so that when the day of evil comes, you may be able to stand your ground, and after you have done everything, to stand. Stand firm then, with the belt of truth buckled around your waist, with the breastplate of righteousness in place, and with your feet fitted with the readiness that comes from the gospel of peace. In addition to all this, take up the shield of faith, with which you can extinguish all the flaming arrows of the evil one. Take the helmet of salvation and the sword of the Spirit, which is the word of God."

—Ephesians 6:13–17

Recently John and I had the flu. That's never a fun time! We were trying to do all the preventive things possible like washing our hands often and taking vitamin C, but we got it anyway. And we even got the flu shot!

Because I am on the computer a lot each week, I am conscious of the germs on my hands transferring to the keyboard and mouse. So when I am sick, I often keep a bottle of rubbing alcohol and cotton pads on my desk to wipe these things down after I have finished, before my husband uses them.

I realize I got that obsessive "Alcohol Attack" from my paternal grandmother, whom my brother and I called Nanie. As a child, I can remember being at her house when she had a cold, and she carried her bottle of rubbing alcohol and tissues around with her all day. If they were not in her hands, they were close by. She would wipe off doorknobs, faucet handles, and fridge handles. Just about everything she touched ultimately got the Alcohol Attack! But it seemed to work. I don't remember anyone in our family ever catching the germs that were causing her to be sick. Looking back on those times, I am very grateful that she took the precautions to protect all of us and combat the evil of the cold or flu with her preventive techniques.

It made me think…what do I do to combat the evil around me, the evil one who is preying on me and wreaking havoc? The Bible, in Ephesians 6:13–17, tells us to put on the full armor of God. Why should we do that? Because these are the things that Satan cannot penetrate.

A friend of mine told me once about a little boy she knows. He is six years old, and every day, when he goes to the closet in his house to put on his coat to go to school, his mom hears him verbally putting on the armor of God. He actually recites the Scripture above! I think I need to take lessons from this little guy and consciously put on my armor of God each morning to protect me throughout the day.

Just my thought for the day…have a blessed one!

Lord, I am so grateful that You provide armor. But not just any armor. This armor can *defeat* the enemy! How wonderful is that? What a gift to me…thank You. Amen.

My Thoughts

16

❖

THE UN-HAPPY BIRTHDAY

"Produce fruit in keeping with repentance."

—Luke 3:8

"First to those in Damascus, then to those in Jerusalem and in all Judea, and to the Gentiles also, I preached that they should repent and turn to God and prove their repentance by their deeds."

—Acts 26:20

"Godly sorrow brings repentance that leads to salvation and leaves no regret, but worldly sorrow brings death. See what this godly sorrow has produced in you: what earnestness, what eagerness to clear yourselves, what indignation, what alarm, what longing, what concern, what readiness to see justice done."

—2 Corinthians 7:10–11a

Sleep-deprived.

That is the only way to describe life with a baby and a toddler. Back in those days, I truly thought I would never sleep again! Both of our precious daughters were getting up at 5:00 a.m. for the day—every day. Maybe not a horrible hour to you, but to me, that is the middle of the night. To say that I am not a morning person is an understatement. I would reluctantly drag myself out of bed and plod down the stairs with these two sweeties at that hour every morning.

They would be wide awake and would love playing together on the floor with their toys while I tried to get the sleep out of my eyes. In addition to not being a morning person, it seems that I would never manage to get to bed at a decent hour, either, so the result was daily sleep deprivation. Sadly, I'm not a coffee drinker, so I was unable to rouse my sleeping body with the stimulants that help America get moving each morning!

A friend advised me once to keep them up later at night so they would sleep later. I did that. They got up even *earlier*! So I quickly returned to the previous bedtime.

On this one particular morning, after an unusually sleepless night, we began, as always, our 5:00 a.m. routine of play and "Mommy wake-up time." And once again, our daughters delightfully played on the floor while I got my sleepy eyes to wake up. Two hours later, I made breakfast and fed Kim in the high chair, with Stephanie beside me at the table eating her toast and bowl of cereal. John came downstairs ready for work. He grabbed his usual bowl of cereal for breakfast, picked up his briefcase, gave his sleepy wife and two playful daughters kisses good-bye, and headed out the door.

I cleaned up the kitchen, dressed the girls, and started my day. It was about two hours later, as I was cleaning the house, that it hit me—it was John's birthday! And I had not even wished him a happy birthday! *Oh, my goodness*! I was in such a sleep-deprived fog that his special day had not even registered in my brain when he left the house. I felt terrible. What an awful thing to not even recognize your husband's birthday.

Of course, I immediately called him at work and wished him a happy day, after I apologized profusely. But I still felt horrible that his day started out as maybe an un-happy birthday. It just does not feel nice when we do wrong things that hurt others, even when they are unintentional. John was gracious and kind, and truthfully, I don't think it even bothered him like it bothered me. But that didn't help me feel any better.

It makes me wonder, do I feel as gut-wrenchingly horrible when I sin against God as I do when I do something to hurt someone else? Sadly, many times, probably not. Wow! I need a real attitude adjustment, don't I? Our sins and truly repentant hearts are good things to reflect on daily.

Just my thought for the day…have a blessed one!

My precious Heavenly Father, I know that not only do I neglect You sometimes, but I even neglect others, sometimes the most important people in my life. Please forgive me, and please wake up my brain when it needs waking. Amen.

My Thoughts

17

GOD'S PURPOSE FOR ME

"Many are the plans in a man's heart, but it is the LORD's purpose that prevails."

—Proverbs 19:21

"And we know that in all things God works for the good of those who love him, who have been called according to his purpose."

—Romans 8:28

"'For I know the plans I have for you,' declares the LORD, 'plans to prosper you and not to harm you, plans to give you hope and a future.'"

—Jeremiah 29:11

I have had several medical issues in my lifetime that required being in the hospital, and in each one, God blessed me with His abundant peace and protection. Recently, it was no different. I had some fluttering and racing of my heart, which I've had at times before. It usually goes away within a short time, but this time I had it for a week, and it didn't look like it was going anywhere. I called the Advice Nurse, and she wanted me to go to Urgent Care for an EKG.

So, at 8:00 on a Monday evening, my husband and I headed up to Kaiser to see what was happening with my heart. I expected that they would give me the test and some instructions and maybe some meds and send me home. I must have been a dreamer because that was not their plan at all! I ended up having to spend the night there and have a lot of tests. Their final determination was that a daily beta blocker would do the trick and finally get my heart beating normally again.

Both of my parents had multiple heart problems for much of their lives, and both died of heart disease. I, too, have had a few heart issues in my life, and I've always known that I seem to have inherited the bad heart gene in our family. Therefore, I try to stay on top of my heart health.

While I was in Urgent Care and pondering all that I would love to do (like every good mulittasker does), I was not only asking God to protect my heart and health; I also was wondering what He might want me to do during the rest of my life on Earth, with my desire being to do things worthwhile and lasting for the kingdom of God. Even with my writing (my devotionals and books), my prayer has always been that God would use them to touch hearts and souls and bring the readers into a closer relationship with Him.

Lately, He has also been speaking to me about possibly starting a ministry for single moms, for which I have a passion. Or maybe He has something else in mind for me to do. I have been praying that He will clearly show me where He wants me to serve. And then I always have questions: "Lord, will You keep me here on Earth long enough to do what You want me to do? Does my life really have a purpose for You? Will You protect my heart so that I may do Your work?"

I got little rest that Monday night. I finally went to sleep very late and woke up every hour. When I did wake, I would pray for a friend who was going in for major surgery the next morning. Then, as I woke up in the early morning light, I realized that I was singing a song in my heart…one that I love and hear often on the radio. I realized that God was speaking to me personally. Here are some of the lyrics to the song "Here for a Reason" by Ashes Remain:

> "Every time that you wake up breathing
> Every night when you close your eyes
> Every day that your heart keeps beating
> There's purpose for your life.
> Every breath that you take has meaning
> You are here for a reason."

God used a song to speak directly to my soul. It's wonderful when He reveals to me how personal He is! After pondering those lyrics, I felt His peace and direction and was confident that He would indeed use me for His will. That morning after I was discharged, my husband and I left the Urgent Care center to drive home. John picked me up at the door, and our favorite Christian radio station was playing on the radio. You would not believe what song was playing as I got in the car. Yes! The song was "Here for a Reason." God showed me once again (in case I missed it the first time!) that every day when I feel my heart beating, it is for His reason, and there is purpose for my life! He has a purpose and plan for every life He creates. He has a purpose and plan for *your* life, too. Praise God!

Just my thought for the day…have a blessed one!

God, why do I ever doubt You? I'm not sure, really. But I thank You that during those times, You always seem to bring it to my attention. I love Your sense of timing, Lord! Amen.

My Thoughts

18

THE DANGERS OF AUTO-CORRECT

"The Spirit helps us in our weakness. We do not know what we ought to pray for, but the Spirit himself intercedes for us with groans that words cannot express. And he who searches our hearts knows the mind of the Spirit, because the Spirit intercedes for the saints in accordance with God's will."

—Romans 8:26–27

"Pray in the Spirit on all occasions with all kinds of prayers and requests. With this in mind, be alert and always keep on praying for all the saints."

—Ephesians 6:18

"Therefore confess your sins to each other and pray for each other so that you may be healed. The prayer of a righteous man is powerful and effective."

—James 5:16

Do you love the smartphones? Actually, there are times I don't think they are very smart at all. Recently my husband and I were at our daughter's house waiting for our grandchildren to come home from school. When we arrived, we noticed that their dog, Georgie, a large Labradoodle, seemed very lethargic, totally uncharacteristic of her. I was thinking she might be sick. Usually when we walk in the door, she greets with lots of "love." But that day, nothing. She never even moved from her comfortable spot on the floor.

I texted Kim with a picture of Georgie and asked if she had been sick. Her answer was no, so I guess Georgie just didn't feel like exerting herself to jump up and down on our behalf that day. A little while later, a neighbor who sometimes helps take care of Georgie stopped by to bring something to Kim. The minute he walked into the house, Georgie, with excitement and reckless abandon, jumped up, ran to the neighbor, and barked and barked with glee! What? That's usually what she does for us! But no worries, we were just happy to see that she wasn't sick after all.

I figured I would contact Kim again so that she knew Georgie was completely healthy. So I texted her this message: "Georgie is fine. Trevor came over, and she joyfully jumped up and barked all over him." Because I usually audio-text, I try to always remember to check it before clicking "send," but I failed to do that this time. Immediately, Kim texted back, "Georgie *barfed* all over Trevor??!! Oh, no! I am so sorry!" I quickly assured her that it was *barked* and that Trevor was fine. But we have had many laughs over that one.

A friend recently told me a story of her phone and auto-correct. Auto-correct can be pretty funny sometimes, like in the story of Georgie. However, my friend's auto-correct story is a little stranger. She said that every time she texts the word "fear," her phone corrects as "great." And when she texts the word "great," it corrects as "fear."

We could say there's a lesson in that for us. When we are

fearful and we begin to pray and call on the name of the Lord Jesus to walk with us in our fear and to release us from the fear, He will do just that. When we reach out to the *great* God of the universe, He is there to calm our fears and help us along the way. What peace we can have when we cast all our fears on Him! So calling on the Lord can actually change our *fear* to *great*!

It's a fact that auto-correct is not perfect, and very often our thoughts get sent wrong because our "not-so-smart" phones miscommunicate our messages. But praise the Lord that our prayers to God *cannot* get miscommunicated! And that is because we have the Holy Spirit to intercede on our behalf so that even our often bungled or confusing words can be sorted out and arrive at His ear in the form of perfect prayers. Praise the Lord!

Just my thought for the day…have a blessed one!

Lord, whenever I am *fearful*, all I have to do is call on You, the *great* God of the universe. Thank You that even my imperfect words and prayers are interceded by the Holy Spirit so that You hear them perfectly. Amen.

My Thoughts

19

GOD'S CLEAN-UP CREW

"He who has clean hands and a pure heart, who does not lift up his soul to an idol or swear by what is false. He will receive blessing from the LORD and vindication from God his Savior. Such is the generation of those who seek him, who seek your face, O God of Jacob."

—Psalm 24:4–6

"I am the true vine, and my Father is the gardener. He cuts off every branch in me that bears no fruit, while every branch that does bear fruit he prunes so that it will be even more fruitful. You are already clean because of the word I have spoken to you. Remain in me, and I will remain in you. No branch can bear fruit by itself; it must remain in the vine. Neither can you bear fruit unless you remain in me."

—John 15:1–4

Before we moved recently, our route to church on Sundays took us down the Clara Barton Parkway near our home. It traveled along the canal and near the Potomac River. It was always a beautiful drive with little traffic and a chance to enjoy the flowers and green trees in the spring and summer and the golden leaves in the fall. The drive also gave us a chance to view the tiny historic old lockhouses, which in days gone by housed the families who tended the canal locks.

Also, we would often see deer leaping along the road and sadly sometimes one that didn't quite make it on its journey down the parkway. One Sunday on our way to church was such a day. But this time, the deer that had likely lost its life as it hit a vehicle, lying right at the edge of the road, was surrounded by ten huge vultures. Some of them were jolted in surprise by our passing car and flew upward, almost hitting our windshield. Others couldn't be bothered by the intrusion and just continued with their meal.

As I watched in amazement how these animals, created by God to be part of the food chain, satisfied their longing for breakfast, I was struck by how, in God's perfect plan, He created some species to have the primary task of being His wildlife "clean-up crew." Isn't it truly awesome that God even planned a way to keep His creation tidy by supplying it with such animals?

But God didn't only supply a clean-up crew for animals and wildlife. He also provided a clean-up crew for us, too— for cleaning up our not-so-tidy sinful selves. Of course, that is Jesus. In God's infinite wisdom, He sent His Son to die for our sins and provide a way for us to spend eternity with Him. We only need to give our lives to Him completely and confess to Him daily the things that need "cleaning up." He also sent the Holy Spirit to be with us here on Earth to guide us in the ways we should live in righteousness with God our Father.

I am forever grateful for God's provision and His "clean-up crew." Praise the Lord!

Just my thought for the day…have a blessed one!

My Lord and Savior, there are so many days that I need cleaning up. I am so grateful that You left me the Holy Spirit and Your Word. May I always recognize my sinfulness and come immediately to You to repent and ask forgiveness. Amen.

My Thoughts

20

THE MOVING BREAKDOWN

"Love is patient, love is kind. It does not envy, it does not boast, it is not proud. It is not rude, it is not self-seeking, it is not easily angered, it keeps no record of wrongs. Love does not delight in evil but rejoices with the truth. It always protects, always trusts, always hopes, always perseveres."

—1 Corinthians 13:4–7

"A man's wisdom gives him patience."

—Proverbs 19:11

"Therefore, as God's chosen people, holy and dearly loved, clothe yourselves with compassion, kindness, humility, gentleness and patience."

—Colossians 3:12

The moving breakdown had nothing to do with the moving van or its contents when we moved to our new home…thankfully. And it had nothing to do with a shattered lamp or broken piece of furniture. We are very grateful that we made it through our move with very few issues.

However, it was my *attitude* that became seriously "broken" a short while after we moved into our new home. Sadly, I admit that I am a member of the "Want It Done Yesterday Club." You know, those obsessive people [*me!*] who want projects completed sooner rather than later or who need everything cleaned up and put away in an *unreasonable* amount of time. I have a hard time tolerating disorder in my own world because it's very distracting to me, so I am clearly one of those people.

I admit that I battle this problem daily. In fact, my dear husband even accuses me of needing to leave the house spit-spot in perfect order for the burglars when we go away on vacation. My need to have everything clean and put away before walking out the door…well, we could call that an obsession. But I tell him it's really because when coming back home with loads of dirty laundry and stuff to put away, the last thing I want is to have a messy and disorganized house, too. But he is quite sure it is to bless the burglars!

Therefore, because I have these expectations of myself, you can imagine that, once we got into our new house, I "wanted everything done yesterday." Therefore, a couple weeks after we moved and had unpacked what seemed like thousands of boxes and put the contents away, I began what I call my "anxiety of perfection." I was intolerable (ask my dear husband!). I was completely impatient and irritable about the length of time it was taking to get settled. I was sure we would never complete the job, and I expressed that often! It felt like we had been in the house *forever*, and it seemed that wherever I looked, I saw things that needed to be done. My husband would always kindly assure me that we would indeed get everything completed, and all would be fine.

However, later that night when I was confessing my sin to

the Lord, He gently showed me something. My mind began to count backward from that day. All of a sudden, I realized that we had been in the house for only *two weeks*! Lord, are You sure it hasn't been two *months*? It certainly feels like it!

And then, when I looked around the house again, I began to focus on the positive, not the negative. I noticed that every room was completely set up, all the furniture was where we wanted it, rugs were down, many pictures had been hung on the walls, kitchen dishes and contents had been shelved, and decorative items were in place. Even some of the curtains were hung. God humbled me as I realized that our house already looked like a home, and it was, what many would say, in perfect order. All but just a few lone boxes had been unpacked. Sure, some pictures and curtains still needed to be hung, but basically the house was pretty much complete.

It is true that I expect more of myself than God ever does. I put more pressure on myself than God ever would do to me. And during these times, He takes advantage of the situation and tries to teach me patience...*with myself*! I am sure He is thinking, "Terry, stop having such high expectations of yourself. Relax, and take time to enjoy *the life I have blessed you with*!"

I know that I can only do that with *His* help. And so daily I must go to the Lord and ask Him for forgiveness and to help me be the woman He created me to be.

Just my thought for the day....have a blessed one!

Heavenly Father, please forgive me for my sin of impatience with myself and others. I am so grateful that You are the sovereign God of the universe, and I am so thankful for Your patience and kindness to me. Amen

My Thoughts

21

From the Deck to the ER

"In his heart a man plans his course, but the LORD determines his steps."

—Proverbs 16:9

"Many are the plans in a man's heart, but it is the LORD's purpose that prevails."

—Proverbs 19:21

"I will instruct you and teach you in the way you should go; I will counsel you and watch over you."

—Psalm 32:8

It was a gorgeous, warm, sunny summer day. I had finished what seemed like a million errands and chores that week. The house was clean, the laundry done, the groceries put away. Dinner had been prepared for our family. And while I was at the store that day, I had purchased a new magazine to read. I had made lemonade, and I poured myself a tall, cool glass. I was by myself at home because our daughters were at school, and John was at work. My plan was to take a break to sit on our deck and read my new magazine. I don't often take time for myself or do random, mundane things to just relax. This was going to be a wonderful afternoon on my deck in the warm sun, drinking cold lemonade and reading.

So, with lemonade in one hand and my magazine tucked safely under my arm, I opened the sliding-glass door and stepped out onto the deck. I slipped out of my flip-flops and took one step toward the lounge chair. At the very moment I put my right foot down on the deck, I felt a searing, cutting pain, the likes of which I had never felt before. I instinctively jerked my foot upward and noticed that I had a larger-than-life piece of wood sticking straight out of the bottom of my heel! We *had* intended to get this very old, splintery deck power-washed, hadn't we?

This piece of wood was about two inches long and as thick as about three toothpicks tied together. It definitely was *not* something that should be sticking out of a foot! Because I was alone, I knew I had to do something quickly, so I reached down and pulled on the hunk of wood. It broke off at the skin line, and I would find out later that a piece about one inch long still remained in my heel. The throbbing rapidly got worse, quickly moving upward until my entire leg was engulfed in agonizing pain. Every cell in my leg seemed to ache and scream *"Help!"*

I called the doctor's office and was told to go right in. By walking on my toes, I was able to get my keys, walk out to the car, and drive to the doctor's office. By now the pain was so bad that it was numbing....and that was probably a good thing. It made it a bit more bearable.

To make a long story short, there was only one thing for the doctor to do—surgery. So I called my husband at work. Because I am allergic to local anesthesia, the doctor sent me to the hospital, and I spent the next several hours in surgery under general anesthesia and then recovery.

Talk about a day gone bad! What happened to my tall glass of ice-cold lemonade and wonderful new magazine?

Do you ever find that sometimes your plans go awry? We can plan and plan, and then "poof"! Something comes along that totally debunks our well-thought-out, completely organized idea. I find that often I think I have my life completely prepared, and then God steps in and says, "Whoa! I don't remember you consulting *Me* first and making your plan in alignment with *Mine*." How arrogant of me, Lord.

I now try to remember to offer each day to God when I wake up and ask Him to lead me, guide me, and show me what *His* plan is. I have to admit, even though unexpected things still sometimes happen, as they always will, my life goes a lot more smoothly when I am in alignment with God's will and I ask Him to go before me each day to bless me with *His* plan.

Just my thought for the day…have a blessed one!

Oh, dear God, *Your* plan is always better than mine. *Always!* But some days I need to get out of my selfish self and trust You for my direction. Amen.

My Thoughts

22

FAITHFUL FRIENDSHIPS

"A friend loves at all times."

—Proverbs 17:17

"A man of many companions may come to ruin, but there is a friend who sticks closer than a brother."

—Proverbs 18:24

"My command is this: Love each other as I have loved you. Greater love has no one than this, that he lay down his life for his friends."

—John 15:12–13

Back when our children were in elementary school, my friend, Cynde, and I used to exercise together by walking each week. We would drop our children off at school at 8:30 in the morning and then meet to begin our walk routine around the neighborhood. It was a wonderful way to keep up with a special friend and an even better way to exercise our bodies. I have fibromyalgia, and exercise is important. Cynde was my encourager and motivator to help me exercise during those years. And our walks included lots of talking, of course! We discussed many things. Parenting things. Mommy things. Spiritual things. Our children's school things. And just plain girl things.

We were our own little support group. We were able to lift one another up when we were feeling discouraged or overwhelmed, and we were able to share joyful experiences and laugh together at the crazy times in our lives. We both had a background in education, we attended the same church, and our children were in the same school. We had a strong common bond.

Having friends is very important. Women especially need friendships and thrive on spending time with other women who can support them on an emotional and personal level. I think one of God's greatest blessings is girlfriends, and He has blessed me with many over the years. I am humbled and grateful for His gift of friendship.

Have you ever noticed how God gives us just the perfect friend to meet a specific need at a specific time in our lives? Friends sometimes come and go. Some are with us for a time and then move away, or we lose touch because our lives follow different paths. But when I look back over my life, I see seasons when God sent me friends who filled a specific need at that time. For instance, when my girls were in elementary school, I needed a mom to share carpooling with. I had no idea how that could possibly work out because no one I knew from the school lived near enough to us to participate together in a carpool. But God had a plan, and over the years He sent a total of four carpool moms to me at different times while my girls were at that school! I was never without a friend to share the driving in all those years.

There were times when I needed a spiritual mentor or someone to walk with me through a time of grief or a difficult and challenging time in my life. There were times that I needed a friend to pray with me, exercise with me, or be a mentor as I raised my children. At every season of my life, and in every specific period of need, God had prepared ahead of time and provided the *perfect* friend to meet that need. And He still does. It is amazing to me how God does that! But He does it. I love friends!

Just my thought for the day…have a blessed one!

Dear Lord, how can I thank You enough for blessing me with beautiful friendships during every season of my life? I have always been able to depend on their faithfulness and love. You have used so many friends to minister to me, and I am so grateful. Amen.

My Thoughts

23

FUZZY WUZZY!

"A cheerful look brings joy to the heart."

—Proverbs 15:30

"I run in the path of your commands, for you have set my heart free."

—Psalm 119:32

"The LORD your God is with you, he is mighty to save. He will take great delight in you; he will quiet you with his love, he will rejoice over you with singing."

—Zephaniah 3:17

Many years ago when I was little, I remember my grandmother's phone when my family and I would travel from Delaware to visit her in Mt. Rainier, Maryland. It was one of those heavy, chunky, now antique, black phones that sat on a table, and it had *no* dial. Of course, today's generation won't even remember the dial! But for many decades, people used rotary phones, which had a dial with holes and numbers under each hole. A person making a phone call would dial the numbers by putting his or her finger in the holes and moving the dial around in a clockwise direction. Our phone at home had numbers, and I would always wonder how in the world my grandmother could call someone without numbers on her phone. But it was simple: she would pick up the receiver, and there would be the telephone operator!

My grandmother would say hello to the operator, who sat somewhere in Mt. Rainier, fielding every call that came through. Now, I don't think there were too many people who had phones in this little town outside Washington, DC, but the operator knew everyone, and she knew every piece of news in the town, too. I'm sure nothing was secret in Mt. Rainier!

My grandmother had a little routine for me when we went to visit. She would have me go into her bedroom, where she had her phone, and she would pick up the receiver to access the operator. Then she would tell the operator that her granddaughter was visiting, and the operator knew where to take it from there. My grandmother would hand me the big, heavy receiver, and I held it to my ear and listened. At that moment, the operator would begin to sing the little song about a bear: "Fuzzy Wuzzy was a bear. Fuzzy Wuzzy had no hair. Fuzzy Wuzzy wasn't fuzzy, was he?" If you're as old as I am, you might remember that jingle, too.

I would just giggle and giggle. I thought that was the funniest thing I had ever heard. Each time I visited my grandmother, in addition to being delighted to spend time with her, I delighted in talking with the operator and hearing "Fuzzy Wuzzy." It was always a fun little "operator moment" that brightened my day!

Isn't it wonderful how God, too, plans little things to delight us? There are so many times during my day when all of a sudden, I will receive a call from a friend, get a card in the mail, see a friendly smile from a stranger in a store, or notice a little flower I had not previously seen along the road. Those are things that bless me immensely and add a special lightness to my day.

Some time ago, my husband and I were out doing errands. I was feeling particularly sad that day, for some reason that I can't even remember now. All I felt like doing was crying inside. We happened to run into a friend in a store and ended up chatting with her for quite some time. By the time we left, I realized that my heart was light, and I felt joyful. I could not stop thanking God for bringing that little moment to my day! He knew that I was sad, so He planned a little "operator moment" to delight my soul to help change that. Praise God for His amazing faithfulness and for caring so much about our feelings!

Just my thought for the day…have a blessed one!

Abba Father, You delight my heart! You bring me joy at just the right times, just when I need it most. Humbly and gratefully, I thank You, Father. Amen.

My Thoughts

24

WALLPAPER BLUNDERS

"Now we know that whatever the law says, it says to
those who are under the law, so that every mouth may be
silenced and the whole world held accountable to God."
—Romans 3:19

"So then, each of us will give an account of himself to God."
—Romans 14:12

"Nothing in all creation is hidden from God's sight.
Everything is uncovered and laid bare before the eyes of
him to whom we must give account."
—Hebrews 4:13

I love creative things, and I especially love decorating our home,
making it a special and comfortable place to live. I enjoy color,
mixing color, matching color, and generally putting things
together to make a pleasant space. And I have always enjoyed
painting rooms in our homes and hanging wallpaper (back
when wallpaper was popular).

Many years ago, I decided to create a little "freshness" in
our family room by painting and hanging a wallpaper border.
There was a chair rail in the room, and we painted different
colors above and below the rail. The wallpaper border I had

picked out with my daughter's help was perfect, we thought. It would tie the two paint colors together nicely and complement the colors in the sofa and chairs. It had a nice design that flowed in one direction.

My daughter was upstairs doing homework, and I began to tackle the wallpaper project. After setting up a long table in the family room and then getting out the paste, brushes, knife, and paper towels, I cut the first piece. This strip of wallpaper was particularly long, and it went around one corner of the room. I slathered on the paste, not too much, not too little. After folding over the ends, I carefully transported it over to the wall and put up the left side, adhering it with a firm swipe of the dry brush. Gently I unfolded the right side and did the same thing to attach it securely to the wall. I wiped the wallpaper with a cloth, ran the dry brush over it one more time, and then ran upstairs and excitedly told Kim to come down and see how good the wallpaper we picked out looked on the wall.

I was so proud of my work because I loved this wallpaper, and it looked great with all the other colors in the room. "Kim, isn't it terrific?"

She took one look and exclaimed, "Mom, it's upside down!" Yikes! Upon closer look, it was indeed upside down. I could not believe I had done that! So down came the wallpaper and back on the table to redo, as Kim bounded back upstairs to do homework. I made sure I had it turned the correct way, evened out the paste a bit, refolded the ends, and then reapplied the paper to the wall. After once again smoothing the paper, wiping off the excess paste, and taking a final look, I ran back upstairs to have Kim come see my project.

As she walked into the room and observed my work, she turned around, looked me straight in the eye, and said, "Mom, you did it *again*! It's upside down!"

OK, given the pattern of the paper, there might be a tiny excuse for applying it wrong once. But *twice*? Seriously! Slowly I humbled myself, took down the paper yet again, and realized that I needed to *focus*. After that, I managed to hang the rest of the paper without incident. For sure, I was very grateful that my daughter was there to catch my mistakes before the glue dried. It's always good to have someone keep us accountable.

It made me think. Do I make sure I have spiritual accountability? Do I make sure that I have Christian friends and relatives come to me when I am not walking the walk? That is much more important than having wallpaper accountability. Many times, with our busy lives and overloaded schedules, we can easily get distracted and not focus on how we are living, or not living, for the Lord. It's very good to have an accountability partner or group of friends to help us stay alert, focused, and on the right path.

Just my thought for the day...have a blessed one!

Lord, please guide me in the way I should go today. If I get off track, help me to be open to Your gentle nudge, Your kind rebuke, or the friends You have placed in my life to keep me accountable. Thank You for loving me enough to keep me on track. Amen.

My Thoughts

25

THE VERY CLEAN BOWL

"Woe to you, teachers of the law and Pharisees, you hypocrites! You clean the outside of the cup and dish, but inside they are full of greed and self-indulgence."
—Matthew 23:25

"Jesus replied, 'I tell you the truth, everyone who sins is a slave to sin.'"
—John 8:34

"Blessed is the man who does not walk in the counsel of the wicked or stand in the way of sinners or sit in the seat of mockers. But his delight is in the law of the LORD, and on his law he meditates day and night."
—Psalm 1:1–2

One of my favorite things to do on a cold and snowy day is to make soup. It just seems like the perfect activity on a chilly day. In fact, not only do I love making soup; I love eating soup, as well. Homemade soup is a very healthy food option. I just made some the other night, even though it wasn't even snowing yet!

One day when I was two years old, I remember my mother making chicken noodle soup for me on a cold winter day. I enjoyed my lunch at the kitchen table…sitting on top of a large phone book so I could reach the soup bowl! Back in the day, being part of the "clean plate club" was admired, and I proudly ate my soup to the last drop.

When I was finished, I remember telling my mother that I had eaten every bit of my soup, and my bowl was *so* clean that she would not even need to wash it. Of course, she said she would wash it anyway because it was still dirty. But my two-year-old mind thought that if I could not *see* the dirt, it was not there. As I looked at the bowl, I could not see one speck of anything, so I insisted that she *not* wash it. I thought I was saving her the extra work, and I remember being so proud of myself for doing that.

After going back and forth with me a few times, I suppose she finally realized the futility of trying to convince a two-year-old. She said yes, it was so clean she didn't need to wash it. However, I was not truly satisfied that she meant it until she opened the cupboard and put the bowl away! Of course, I know now that later, when I wasn't looking, she took it out and washed it, but I did not know that then. It was kind of her to play along.

You know, sometimes it is easy for us to ignore our sins and look at the "bowl" of our lives and think it is clean. Oh, how foolish! The God of the universe knows full well, just like my mother did, that our bowls are not clean, but instead are filled with the dirt and messiness of our sin. That's why it is so important that we go to our heavenly Father each day and confess our less-than-admirable behaviors to Him. He is just waiting, like the loving Father He is, to forgive us. What a wonderful thought!

Just my thought for the day…have a blessed one!

There is so much to battle these days, Lord. I cannot do it without You. Please give me Your strength to battle my sinful self and focus on Your Word. Amen.

My Thoughts

26

❖◆❖

THE GENTLEMEN OF TRASH

"Now we ask you, brothers, to respect those who work hard among you, who are over you in the Lord and who admonish you."

—1 Thessalonians 5:12

"Show proper respect to everyone: Love the brotherhood of believers, fear God, honor the king."

—1 Peter 2:17

"A kindhearted woman gains respect."

—Proverbs 11:16

I have many fond memories of my grandparents from when I was growing up. Both my grandmothers had an enormous impact on my life, and I am forever grateful to them for the time they spent with me. Sometimes they had specific wisdom to impart or stories to tell. I "caught" other life lessons when I witnessed their behavior during everyday situations.

One of those lessons taught to me by my paternal grandmother, Nanie, was respect—respect for everyone in society, especially those who are not "high society" or those whom others might look down on. My grandmother lived just across the line from Washington, DC, in a very modest home in Mt. Rainier, Maryland. She had an alley behind her house that was used, among other things, by the trash-truck drivers to access each neighbors' backyard and to collect the trash each week.

Not only did Nanie give the trash collectors gifts each year at Christmas and also converse with them many times when they drove down her alley, but I remember that she always referred to them as "the *gentlemen* who collect my trash." Wow! I can still hear her sweet voice in my mind saying that. She did not use that word to impress me or anyone else. She did not use that word in a condescending way. She did not use that word to make people feel that she was superior by calling them gentlemen. It was a result of exactly how she thought about these men. In her heart, they *were* gentlemen, and she respected them and was grateful for the work they did for her each week.

She had a keen respect for all God's creations, and I caught that attitude loud and clear. I sensed her kindness to others, her love of people, and her gratitude for them and their work ethic, all by listening to her as she referred to these men as gentlemen. She was blessed by them, but I believe they were blessed by her, as well. They had to feel her love and respect.

To this day, when I see trash collectors, I think of Nanie in casual conversation referring to the "gentlemen who collect my trash." That left an enormous impression on me. And you know....they *were* gentlemen. In turn, they treated my grandmother with a great deal of respect, as well.

God created each of us to have value, regardless of our jobs, our social status, or our handicaps. We have value because we were created in the image of God and because God loves us.

God commands us many times in the Bible to respect others, whether it's our parents, our spouses, our neighbors, or workers in the Lord. Wouldn't the world be a wonderful place if we treated everyone in our lives with that measure of respect?

Just my thought for the day…have a blessed one!

Heavenly Father, I don't like it when others are rude to me. So why do I allow myself to be rude to people sometimes? Please help me in my weakness, Lord. Amen.

My Thoughts

27

OFF-KEY

"Give thanks to the LORD, call on his name; make known among the nations what he has done.
Sing to him, sing praise to him; tell of all his wonderful acts.
Glory in his holy name; let the hearts of those who seek the LORD rejoice."

—1 Chronicles 16:8–10

"But I, with a song of thanksgiving, will sacrifice to you. What I have vowed I will make good. Salvation comes from the LORD."

—Jonah 2:9

"This is the day the LORD has made; let us rejoice and be glad in it."

—Psalm 118:24

When I was young, I sang in the youth choir at our church. I'm not exactly sure why that was so because I could not even carry a tune in a bucket, as they used to say. I recall being mortified one week at practice when the choir director asked me to sing a few lines as a solo. Wisely, she quickly realized that would never work and that I would bring much harm to the hymn we were singing that week.

She moved on to another voice for that part, and that was

a good decision. I think it was my mother's dream to have her children sing in the church choir, so without a choice, sing I did. Or should I say, I *attempted* to sing! I truly feel that the day I "outgrew" the youth choir was a good day for the church! I never moved on to the adult choir.

Years later, I remember the pastor at our new church being a bit frustrated because the people in the congregation would not sing…at least not to his liking, which was loud enough for all to hear. He began telling the people each week that the voice they had was the one that God created for them, and that if God created it, God loved it, and we should all praise Him with the voices we had been given. And praise Him loud enough to be heard. I was thinking, "But you have not heard *my* voice!"

To this day, I have no musical talent, but the truth is, I have always wished I did. I used to dream as a child about being on stage, singing and dancing. And that's another story because I do not have a coordinated bone in my body, either! I am hoping that part of my duties in heaven will include singing in the heavenly choir because at that time, of course, I will have my new voice!

How do you praise God? Do you sing with all your heart in church? Do you sing in the choir? Do you praise Him at home, singing while you work? Do you sing with the radio, or do you whisper praises to Him throughout the day? No matter how you praise God, the important thing is to *do* it! God loves it when we use our voices in whatever way He directs us to worship and praise Him for all that He is and all that He does in our lives!

Singing may not be my gift, but I can still use my voice to praise God in ways that are glorifying to Him.

Just my thought for the day…have a blessed one!

I know that not having the gift of singing or music does not let me off the hook, God! I love to praise You and all that You are. And I need to use the gifts that You have given me to glorify You as often as I can. Amen.

My Thoughts

28

TRAFFIC CHAOS

"O LORD, my strength and my fortress, my refuge in time of distress, to you the nations will come from the ends of the earth and say, 'Our fathers possess nothing but false gods, worthless idols that did them no good.'"

—Jeremiah 16:19

"God is light; in him there is no darkness at all. If we claim to have fellowship with him yet walk in the darkness, we lie and do not live by the truth."

—1 John 1:5–6

"I will instruct you and teach you in the way you should go; I will counsel you and watch over you."

—Psalm 32:8

The other day, I was driving home after sharing the afternoon with a friend. Washington, DC-area traffic is usually horrendous at best, especially around the times of "rush hour," which this happened to be. As in any metropolitan area, it is often very congested and noisy. That day, amid the blaring of horns and the roar of speeding traffic, I heard a familiar sound nearby. The piercing sirens of fire emergency vehicles seemed to come out of nowhere.

At the time, I was preparing to pass through a large, congested intersection, crossing six lanes, with nowhere to pull over. I quickly looked in my rearview mirror and around me. No flashing lights. The sound seemed to be coming from my right, but I saw no emergency vehicles or fire trucks there. As I made my way amid heavy traffic, I quickly looked ahead and to my left. Nothing there, either. But the noise was coming closer.

It is sometimes difficult to identify immediately the direction of the sirens when you are so distracted and preoccupied with all that is going on around you as you maneuver through traffic. I was driving in six lanes of heavy traffic, traversing across another six lanes at the intersection, with dozens of cars to my left and behind and ahead of me. Although it was nothing unusual for our area's traffic, it was still distracting. I also had a huge commuter bus on my right, and the driver was trying to move into my lane, merging in to my lane ahead of me. Cars from my left were also trying to merge into my lane to get onto the freeway just ahead. All while I was trying to determine where the emergency vehicles were coming from.

After I crossed the six lanes to the other side, I again looked in my rearview mirror. There they were, almost upon me! A huge hook-and-ladder fire truck and another fire emergency vehicle, lights blazing! I immediately pulled over, along with all the other drivers who had evidently not seen them until now, either. It is hard to hear over all the other traffic noises.

This chaos is nothing new for the Washington, DC, area. In fact, until recently, we were given the distinct "honor" of having the worst traffic congestion in the entire country! For sure, being number one in traffic congestion is *not* something any place aspires to be noted for! Thankfully, Los Angeles has now taken that award from us, and we are quite happy to let them have it. However, when I look at our traffic situation in DC today, I am not likely to notice the difference!

Have you ever missed the warning signs of impending danger that was coming your way? Do you sometimes have so many distractions and preoccupations around you that you miss the possibility of being involved in a harmful situation completely? Do you sometimes let the noise and chaos in life keep you from spending time with the King of kings and Lord of lords? Along with prayer and meditating on the Scriptures, spending time with our Savior is the most important thing we can do to protect ourselves from the evil one, Satan, who comes to distract, destroy, and deplete us. In the same way that we have to keep our eyes focused on the road when we drive and pay attention 100 percent of the time, we must also pay attention to our spiritual lives, too.

What is the most distracting thing for you that keeps you from spending time with the Lord?

Just my thought for the day....have a blessed one!

Oh, my precious Lord, I am so sorry that sometimes I take You for granted...I ignore You because I think You will always be there. And actually, You *will* always be there, but no one likes to be taken for granted, and it is a sin for me to do that. Please forgive me, Lord. Amen.

My Thoughts

29

SHOPPING HELPER

"For he has rescued us from the dominion of darkness and brought us into the kingdom of the Son he loves, in whom we have redemption, the forgiveness of sins."
—Colossians 1:13–14

"But you are a forgiving God, gracious and compassionate, slow to anger and abounding in love."
—Nehemiah 9:17

"Who is a God like you, who pardons sin and forgives the transgression of the remnant of his inheritance? You do not stay angry forever but delight to show mercy. You will again have compassion on us; you will tread our sins underfoot and hurl all our iniquities into the depths of the sea."
—Micah 7:18–19

When my now-adult daughter was two years old, she and I would go grocery shopping each week together while her older sister was in kindergarten. Kim was very friendly, and as she rode in the grocery-cart seat, she would spend her time chatting with every shopper who passed us in the aisles. She would always say hello to them, even if they were deep in thought over their massive grocery lists. If they failed to say hello back, she would talk to them until they did.

By the time I would finish my shopping, it seemed that we knew everyone in the grocery store! It was always a joyful time, and most people loved to chat with a friendly two-year-old.

Just like all the other shoppers, I, too, was deep in thought on this particular day as I compared prices, shopped with my coupons, and read labels. I had loaded the cart with items from the produce section and the dairy section, and I was now pondering items in the cereal aisle. When I turned around to put a box of cereal in the cart, Kim, with a sparkle in her eyes and a helpful-looking smile on her face, handed me the egg carton from our cart…the *empty* egg carton!

After I caught my breath, all I could think of was how in the world I was going to clean up the gooey mess as I imagined all my groceries soaked and dripping with a dozen raw eggs. The woman shopping next to me just chuckled and proceeded on. I was imagining the loudspeaker with its piercing voice yelling, "Cleanup in aisle three—a dozen broken, gooey eggs!"

I was ready to begin dealing with this yucky task, and then to my surprise, when I looked in our cart, *not one egg had broken* when Kim dumped them from the carton! I am sure it was God taking pity on me because I cannot imagine how they could have all still been in one piece. But I was certainly very grateful.

Have you ever been in a situation where you were certain that something you did was going to result in utter failure? Have you ever made a mistake, fully anticipating the consequence, and then you found in the end that things turned out perfectly fine? There are even times when our mistakes actually lead us to a better result than we would have had originally.

There are many examples in the Bible of people who made

bad choices, but in the end, God redeemed them. Look at David and his affair with Bathsheba and then consequently murdering her husband. Wow! That hardly seems redeemable, does it? But after David repented, God used him in a big way.

God, in His infinite mercy and grace, will forgive all who come to Him with repentant hearts. The key is to ask God to reveal our sins to us if we have not acknowledged them already, and then come before Him in total submission and repentance and ask His forgiveness. He will not turn from us when we are sincere; instead, He will forgive us and heal us. Praise His name!

Just my thought for the day…have a blessed one!

Honestly, Lord, sometimes I just feel like a total failure. Utterly unredeemable, really. But what amazes me is that when I repent and ask forgiveness, You, with Your big strong arms, come to me, lift me out of my self-created slime, and redeem me! Thank You, Lord! Amen.

My Thoughts

30

THE CHERRY TREE

"But grow in the grace and knowledge of our Lord and
Savior Jesus Christ. To him be glory both now and forever!
Amen."

—2 Peter 3:18

"Preach the Word; be prepared in season and out of season;
correct, rebuke and encourage—with great patience and
careful instruction."

—2 Timothy 4:2

"There is a time for everything, and a season for every
activity under heaven."

—Ecclesiastes 3:1

Several years ago, we planted a small Japanese Cherry Tree in
our backyard. I had always wanted a cherry tree because I love
their delicate, beautiful blossoms, and they are well-known for
being the "signature" Washington, DC, tree. Dozens of them
adorn the area surrounding the Tidal Basin downtown, as well
as throughout the city and metro area.

Our little tree was small and scrawny, but I loved it. It
seemed as though it might take forever to grow big enough
to truly make a statement in our backyard. Eleven years later,
it commanded a beautiful presence, along with the two crepe

myrtles and the flowers on our patio. I think our tree is majestic, and with its large, perfect shape, it is just beginning to hang over our patio, where it shades our swing, my favorite place to sit and pray on a sunny day.

I have taken many photos of our tree...breathtaking blossoms in the spring, golden leaves in the fall, and even branches laden with snow in the winter. This tree makes me happy. But more importantly, it makes me feel close to God. I see God's glory in each season that passes as our tree grows, changes, and beautifies our yard.

It's somewhat like our spiritual lives. We accept Jesus as our personal Savior and are "planted" to begin growing. Our growth goes through many changes, seasons, and challenges as we strive to become the men and women God created us to be. We have seasons of new growth and seasons of bareness. We sometimes blossom in a spiritual boost like the gorgeous, delicate blossoms of the cherry tree. Then at other times, we shine with God's glory like the golden leaves of fall. Even other times may be opportunities to just quietly listen to God.

Just like the tree, God uses each season to transform us, grow us, or use us to achieve His purpose in our lives. He may use us to spread His message, to share His love with others, or serve in myriad ways. But in each case, in each season, God is growing us and shaping us to be in His perfect will.

Isn't it wonderful to know that we have an omnipresent, omnipotent God who not only loves us more than we can ever imagine, but who walks with us through our spiritual seasons as we move toward a full relationship with Him? That is a big reason to praise Him each morning!

Just my thought for the day…have a blessed one!

Dear Jesus, sometimes growing is painful.
Sometimes I don't even feel like growing! But
the truth is, if I will grow with You, Lord, my
relationship with You will be awesome! Amen.

My Thoughts

31

CONFESSIONS OF MY "UN"

"When they kept on questioning him, he straightened up and said to them, 'If any one of you is without sin, let him be the first to throw a stone at her.'"

—John 8:7

"But God demonstrates his own love for us in this: While we were still sinners, Christ died for us."

—Romans 5:8

"For God so loved the world that he gave his one and only Son, that whoever believes in him shall not perish but have eternal life."

—John 3:16

When my granddaughter was little, she would often exclaim, "This is *the best* day of my life!" on occasions when something wonderful happened or when there was a special surprise or event in her life. I always loved hearing those sweet words when she made her pronouncement. She was so innocent and so grateful for the special little, and big, blessings that God brought her way. Her shout of "This is *the best* day of my life!" was her way of thanking Him for His gifts to her.

Like my granddaughter, I have often said the same thing about the sermons/messages that our pastors preach in our church each week. Every Sunday for the past several years, I have come out of church saying, "That was *the best* sermon!" We have heard many wonderful messages in the churches we have attended. We have absorbed a treasure trove of solid biblical teaching and application and have been mightily blessed.

A recent service was no different, and the message, once again, did not disappoint. Our pastor spoke about the passage in Luke 7:36–50 about the woman who washed Jesus's feet with her tears and anointed Him with her expensive perfume. Our pastor did an amazing job of prefacing his message with an entire history lesson of customs and life during the time when Jesus walked the earth and how they impacted this scene with the Pharisee, the woman, and Jesus. More importantly, he taught about the Pharisee's sinfulness, the woman's sinfulness, and Jesus's love. Jesus admonished the Pharisee for his judgmental attitude, and although the woman had lived a very sinful life, it was her convicting faith in Jesus, her devotion to Him, and giving her life to Him that caused Jesus to say to her, "Your sins are forgiven."

The pastor showed us that many times, we are very unlovable—uncaring, unfaithful, unworthy, unhelpful, unkind, ungodly, unappealing, uncharitable, unfair—and on and on. *But* we are *never unloved.* We might be *un*-everything, but in spite of our sinfulness, we are *always* loved by God.

As I listened to our pastor, I was brutally convicted of my own sinfulness, all my "uns." I think of how many times I excuse my sinfulness, rationalize my sinfulness, and feel self-righteous because at least I "don't act like that horrible person." Even if I don't voice it, in my heart of hearts, I know it's there.

Forgive me, Lord, for my self-righteousness and pride.

And God revealed to me how "un" I am when I judge others based on what I perceive as *their* sinfulness. In God's eyes, every sin has the same degree of evil. That's often a hard concept to swallow. One sin is not "less" and another "more." Sin is sin in God's eyes, and He doesn't care about the degree. He cares about my heart. And when I judge another's heart and consider myself better, *that alone is sin. Forgive me, Lord*, for my pride. For my arrogance. For my self-righteousness. I know, Lord, that You sent Your son to die for those people, too!

I pray that I will not be unkind, uncaring, ungodly, or uncharitable and that instead, I will be kind, loving, and giving. And most of all, I pray that I would be patient. Just like You are patient with me, Lord.

As I was paging through some poems God wrote through me a year ago, one stood out. It seems to fit perfectly with what our pastor was sharing. In His mercy, God gently reminded me through this poem that He put on my heart the same message that was shared in our church. God has a way of humbling me at just the right times! Thank You, Lord!

(Please see the poem titled "Your Love" at the end of this book.)

Just my thought for the day…have a blessed one!

You know, it makes me realize how very, very grateful and thankful I am, Lord, that You don't look at me in the same way I sometimes look at others! Thank You, Lord, for Your mercy and forgiveness. Amen.

My Thoughts

32

My Baby Brother

"Now to him who is able to do immeasurably more than all we ask or imagine, according to his power that is at work within us, to him be glory in the church and in Christ Jesus throughout all generations, for ever and ever! Amen."

—Ephesians 3:20–21

"I will bless them and the places surrounding my hill. I will send down showers in season; there will be showers of blessing."

—Ezekiel 34:26

When I was two and a half years old, my brother was born. I can vividly remember the day my parents brought him home from the hospital. There was a bassinet in the living room just waiting for this new little life to be placed where all in attendance would lovingly "Ooooh" and "Ahhhh" at his appearance. I knew a baby brother was coming to our house, and I was quite excited in my own little two-year-old way, although I had no idea what to expect.

My parents and grandparents had prepared me for this event. Back in those days, when a woman gave birth, she spent *two weeks* in the hospital afterward. So, because my father was at work each day, I had been staying with my grandmothers, taking turns spending time with them at their homes. I had been anxiously waiting this arrival but very uncertain of what all this would look like, having a new baby in the house.

So, with both my grandmothers, in our little one-bedroom apartment, we gathered on this day of homecoming. It seemed like forever, but when my parents arrived and placed my brother in his little bed, I immediately went over to it and peeked over the edge to look at this new person who had come to live with us. I can remember barely being tall enough to peer over the side of the bassinet to see what was inside.

And as I looked at him for the first time, I remember exclaiming in surprise, "He has fingers! He has eyes! He has a mouth! He has a nose!" I continued to shout in amazement at each little part of him, and all four adults stood around the bassinet laughing at the surprise in my voice over this bundle they had brought home. My mother told me years later that she's not sure *what* I thought was coming home to live with us, but, clearly, I did not realize it was going to be a *human baby*!

Have you ever been surprised at a gift you received? Did you think it was going to be something nice, and then you were blessed with something that far exceeded your expectations? I think that's how God loves to bless us. Sometimes in our prayers, we ask God for something, and then instead of giving us what we prayed for, He gives us exceedingly more than we ask or imagine! I think that, like earthly parents, He is so pleased, and it brings Him joy to bless us in ways that surprise us and that we would never dream.

Just my thought for the day…have a blessed one!

Lord, many days when I least expect it, You give me a special little blessing. Sometimes I have to look for it, but it is there. Thank You, Lord, for unexpected blessings. Amen.

My Thoughts

33

QUIET IN CHURCH

"Shout for joy to the LORD, all the earth. Worship the
LORD with gladness; come before him with joyful songs."
—Psalm 100:1–2

"Likewise, the tongue is a small part of the body, but it
makes great boasts. Consider what a great forest is set on
fire by a small spark. The tongue also is a fire, a world of
evil among the parts of the body. It corrupts the whole
person, sets the whole course of his life on fire, and is itself
set on fire by hell."
—James 3:5–6

"With the tongue we praise our Lord and Father, and with
it we curse men, who have been made in God's likeness.
Out of the same mouth come praise and cursing. My
brothers, this should not be. Can both fresh water and salt
water flow from the same spring? My brothers, can a fig
tree bear olives, or a grapevine bear figs? Neither can a salt
spring produce fresh water."
—James 3:9–12

As a very young child, I remember going to church with my
mother one Sunday and sitting with her in the church pew.
I'm not sure why on this particular Sunday I was in the church
sanctuary with her instead of in my usual Sunday School class,

but I do remember that we sat near the front. I suppose it was so she could provide a way for me to see more easily.

After the worship and singing, the pastor began to preach. From a child's perspective, he looked to be standing very high above us in his podium at the altar. It seemed as though he was on top of a huge mountain looking down at us. I remember nothing at all about anything he said, but I do remember that he was speaking very loudly at times—shouting, really, as preachers sometimes do when they are passionately preaching the word of God.

At one point, I looked at my mother and said, probably in a louder-than-desired voice, "Why is that man yelling at us?" My mother mumbled something to me in a whisper and then mostly said "Shhhhh."

As a young child, I could only relate his shouting to an angry parent or teacher, or to a child who was being mean to another child. It never occurred to me that someone might shout with joy or with excitement when speaking of Jesus. I would learn that later.

In the book of James, we are told much about the tongue. James says, "All kinds of animals, birds, reptiles and creatures of the sea are being tamed and have been tamed by man, but no man can tame the tongue." He also says, "With the tongue we praise our Lord and Father, and with it we curse men, who have been made in God's likeness. Out of the same mouth come praise and cursing" (James 3:7–10)

What James said centuries ago is still true today. Our tongues can be used for good or for bad. It is our choice. It is so easy to say something rude, unkind, or mean in a moment of anger, and we can never take those words back. It is good to take a deep breath before responding to someone's attacks and ask the Holy Spirit to help us with the response He would have us give. Or maybe no response at all.

Just my thought for the day...have a blessed one!

Dear Lord, my tongue is so powerful, and it has the ability to encourage, praise, bless, honor, and bring joy. I am ashamed that it also has the ability to hurt others deeply. Please forgive me for those times, Lord, and bring restoration. Amen.

My Thoughts

34

❖❖❖

MUD PIES AND AIRPLANES

"Jesus said, 'Let the little children come to me, and do not hinder them, for the kingdom of heaven belongs to such as these.'"

—Matthew 19:14

"Even a child is known by his actions, by whether his conduct is pure and right."

—Proverbs 20:11

"He called a little child and had him stand among them. And he said: 'I tell you the truth, unless you change and become like little children, you will never enter the kingdom of heaven. Therefore, whoever humbles himself like this child is the greatest in the kingdom of heaven.'"

—Matthew 18:2–4

When I was a young child, my neighbor friend and I would play for endless hours in my backyard. It was just a small-town, country backyard. No landscaping. No lush green grass watered weekly. Pretty much nothing but crabgrass and weeds, and in one part of the yard nearest the house, there was nothing but dirt. Oh, but this was play heaven for little children! Because my parents didn't mind that things got a little messed up in the backyard or that we used it for our imaginative play, it provided a spot each day where our fantasies could take hold and wonderful, exciting adventures could result.

One of the things we loved doing the most was baking mud pies. We would spend hours and hours digging in the dirt, retrieving water from the hose, stirring the mixture, and then forming "cakes." Sometimes we would even add special "ingredients" or decorations on top of leaves, sticks, and small stones. After that, we would place the mud pies in our makeshift oven, which we had made from old pieces of wood that we found along the way. There our cakes would bake in the sun all morning.

Once we were sure they were completely done and ready to serve, we would remove them from the oven and place them on little plates to be part of our imaginary meal. I will leave it there and won't go into detail about how we sometimes actually *took bites* of these beautiful delicacies that we served at our little luncheons!

One of our other enjoyable backyard adventures was building little airplanes from pieces of wood, likely the same wood that we used to make our ovens for mud pies. We would hammer away, and after we made sure our planes were secure and air-worthy, we would dig up large, fat earthworms from the soil and place them aboard these vehicles of flight, running with them lifted high in our hands and gliding them all over our yard and neighborhood, I'm sure at the violent objection of these poor earthly creatures! Eventually, however, we did return them to their moist homes in the soil.

Isn't the creativity of children amazing? They don't worry about things like getting their clothes dirty, making the yard a mess, the danger of eating nasty mud pies, forcing earthworms to fly, or getting hurt. That's what is so wonderful about children. They are completely innocent and easily become absorbed in their world of fantasy and creative play. Sadly, sometimes this world today robs them of their innocence because it often moves too fast and wants them to grow up at breakneck speed. And that is so unfortunate because they are young for such a short time.

Jesus thought about the innocence of children, too. He often demonstrated that He was more than delighted to spend time with them, even at the expense of the adults in the group. He would listen to their questions, and at an unhurried pace, He would take joy in answering them. He even went so far as to say that the kingdom of heaven belongs to them! And then if that wasn't enough, He had the boldness to say, "Unless you change and become like little children, you will never enter the kingdom of heaven."

Wow! That sounds like something we should pay attention to. Just my thought for the day…have a blessed one!

Lord, when my brain gets all wrapped up in
the complications of life, help me step back and
remember my childhood and then come to You
with that pure and simple faith of a child. I know
You are waiting for me. Amen.

My Thoughts

35

WHERE WILL YOU LIVE?

"For God so loved the world that he gave his one and only Son, that whoever believes in him shall not perish but have eternal life."

—John 3:16

"Jesus said to her, 'I am the resurrection and the life. He who believes in me will live, even though he dies; and whoever lives and believes in me will never die.'"

—John 11:25–26

I have had many problems with sciatic nerve pain, and during some of those times, I could hardly move. And also during those times, I was blessed to have a chiropractor who patiently worked with me, gave me exercises to do, guided me, and managed to get me to the point where I have virtually no pain. In addition, I had many friends and family praying for me and for my freedom from pain and healing of my sciatic nerve. I am very, very grateful. There were times when I did not think I would get to this point, and I am thrilled to have pain-free mobility again!

One day when I was in my chiropractor's office, I noticed a sign hanging on the wall. It simply said this:

If you don't take care of your body, where will you live?

I had to laugh…it was so thought-provoking in a funny kind of way. But when I seriously considered it, the idea really made me stop and think. I was struck not only by the simplicity of the question but with the *power* of the question. And as I pondered that, and the fact that we are indeed given only one body, it reinforced yet again the importance of taking care of our bodies, taking care of ourselves, getting exercise, eating healthy foods, and staying away from things that would be harmful to our bodies. Yes, this one body has to last a while!

As I continued to ponder this sign, I realized that we also need to ask the next logical question: "If you don't take care of your soul, where will you live for all eternity?" My pastor often reminds us that *everyone* will live for eternity. The only question is, "Where?"

Have you ever thought about that? Have you ever pondered the question about where you will live for all eternity? The Bible tells us there are really only two options, and we will each live in one of them. Because of its eternal implications, that question is an even deeper and more important question than where you will live right now.

One of the options, of course, is spending eternity with Jesus in heaven. But what must we do to have the confidence and be *guaranteed* that we indeed will live forever with Jesus in heaven? God's response, His answer, is in the Bible. It tells us clearly that we need to recognize that we are sinful people. Just doing good things and not murdering someone does not mean that we are not sinful. The Bible tells us in 1 John 1:8–9, "If we claim to be without sin, we deceive ourselves and the truth is not in us. If we confess our sins, He is faithful and just and will forgive us our sins and purify us from all unrighteousness."

We must first recognize that we need a Savior. We must believe that Jesus is the Son of God, who died for our sins, and believe that He was raised from the dead and that we will be, too, if we trust Him and give our lives to Him in this life.

It's pretty simple, really, just like the question about where we will live now. Simple. It is simple to take care of our bodies, but we must just do it. It is simple to take care of our souls, too, but we must just do it. It does take faith and a deliberate action to give our lives to Jesus, but He will help us navigate through this difficult world in a much better way than we could navigate it ourselves.

I am so very grateful that I made the choice years ago to put Jesus at the helm of my life. And when I stay in tune with Him through prayer and reading the Bible and meditating on His Word, then the things in my life go a lot more smoothly. And even when they don't and they become chaotic or overwhelming, God is there to give me the strength I need to get through it. And for that I am very, very grateful!

Just my thought for the day…have a blessed one!

Precious Jesus, I want to live with You for all eternity. I confess to You that I am a sinner and in need of Your saving grace. I ask that You please forgive me for all my sins, and I humbly come before You and give You my heart and my life. Thank You for giving Your life in order to make it possible for me to have salvation and live forever with You. Amen.

My Thoughts

Your Love
By Terry Harris

Thank you, Lord, for Your love for me!
Your love is far beyond what I can comprehend
It is unconditional
Faithful
Longsuffering
Your love is wider than the universe
It is strong
Beautiful
Dependable
It is comforting
Assuring
Warm
Your love is greater than my mind can imagine
It is higher than the heavens
And higher still

And yet…
It is right here with me
Always
Forever
For me.

Forgive me, Lord, when I don't love You back
When I leave You on the sidelines to long for me
While I go about my busyness
I cast You aside to make room for me
I take for granted that You will be there
Because I know You will never leave me
Forgive me, Lord.

I love You, Lord
My love is so small compared to Your love for me
Minutiae compared to the vastness of Your love
I do love You, Lord, with all my tiny little heart
You are my rock
You are my all
I love You so.

NOTE FROM THE AUTHOR

God blesses us in so many different ways—ways that personally speak directly to our hearts and souls. Ways that speak only to us. He knows us so intimately and loves us so deeply that He can tailor His words to us through many different sources. I pray that during your reading of The Warmth of the SON, you felt God's presence in the personal way in which He speaks to you and that you could hear His voice calling to you as you turned the pages of this book. May your heart be blessed with the goodness of His love.

Blessings,

Terry

authorterryharris@gmail.com

ABOUT THE AUTHOR

Terry is a wife, mother and grandmother who shares her life experiences through her words of rhyme. Like others, she has lived life's joys as well as painful trials, and it is through these experiences that Terry has found the inspiration for her poetry.

In addition to writing inspirational poetry, she also enjoys writing whimsical rhyme for children, which can be seen in the children's picture books she has published. Terry loves writing poetry and has written since she was a child.

Terry taught elementary school and pre-school for 15 years in the Washington, DC area and owned a scrapbooking business for 23 years. She now enjoys her new career writing and publishing. Her favorite interests are her family and grandchildren, her church, running a ministry for single moms and their children, reading, amateur photography, preserving her family faith stories, writing, traveling with friends and family and creating note cards with her photos and poems. Terry and her husband John recently moved from the Washington, DC area to Washington state.

Other books by Terry Harris:

Eat Your Colors!—A rhyming picture book for young children about eating healthy, colorful foods

Oh My, Dear Me, Gee Whiz!—A whimsical rhyming picture book for young children about animals

A Friend, A Friend, That's What I Am!—A whimsical rhyming book for young children about friendship

I Love Jesus, Jesus Loves Me!—A charming little colorful book of devotions for young children. Includes a short scripture verse for you and your child to say together, a short lesson with interactive questions, fun activities, and a prayer to pray for your child.

Do You Hear a Rhyme?—A delightful book for young children filled with poems and beautiful illustrations. Some poems are silly and some are serious, but each will capture the hearts of the children who hear them.

Breathe with Thee: Poems from the Heart of God—Inspirational poetry, Scripture, and photos

Grace Upon My Heart: Poems of an Awesome God!—Inspirational poetry, Scripture, and photos. Could be described as Volume 2 of *Breathe with Thee*.

The Warmth of the SON—A devotional series containing stories about God's faithfulness, grace, and mercy in the simple things of life

The Bridge That God Built—how a single moms ministry refreshes, supports, loves, and encourages single moms and their children. Amazing story of how God is clearly in control of every detail of our lives, and when we are inside His perfect will, He will bless our efforts beyond measure and meet our every need.

The Voice within My Soul—inspirational poetry, scripture and photos. A compilation of Breathe with Thee and Grace Upon My Heart, but with many additional poems, scripture and photos.

All Terry's books can be found on Amazon.com

You can contact Terry through the following:

- Email: authorterryharris@gmail.com
- Website: www.authorterryharris.com
- Blog: terhar.wordpress.com

Made in the USA
Middletown, DE
16 October 2022

12859959R00093